In The Hands of My Enemy

One Woman's Story
of World War II

In
The Hands
of
My Enemy

One Woman's Story
of World War II

Sigrid Heide

English Translation
by Norma Johansen
as arranged
by Ethel Keshner

Southfarm Press, Publisher
Middletown, Connecticut

Originally published under the title *Kanskje i morgen--* by H. Aschehoug & Co. (W. Nygaard), Oslo, Norway in 1946.

Republished in Norway in 1995 by Exil Forlag A/S, Halden.

...ited States of America in 1996 by Southfarm Press/Haan ...hing Services, Ltd., Middletown, Connecticut.

Southfarm Press, Publisher

Haan Graphic Publishing Services, Ltd.

P.O. Box 1296

Middletown, Connecticut 06457

Library of Congress Cataloging-in-Publication Data

Heide, Sigrid

    [[Kanskje i morgen. English]

    In the hands of my enemy : one woman's story of World War

II / Sigrid Heide ; English translation by Norma Johansen ; as

arranged by Ethel Keshner.

        p.   cm.

    ISBN 0-913337-29-3 (hardcover)

    1. Heide, Sigrid. 2. World War, 1939-1945--Prisoners and prisons,

German. 3. World War, 1939-1945--Underground movements--Norway.

4. Prisoners of war--Germany--Biography. 5. Prisoners of war--Norway

--Biography. 6. World War, 1939-1945--Personal narratives,

Norwegian. 7. Norway--History--German occupation, 1940-1945.

I. Title.

D805.G3H36513 1996

940.54'7243'092--dc20

[B]   96-34888

                                          CIP

Printed in The United States of America

Introduction

Sigrid Heide was born in Halden, Norway, the seventh of nine children. When the Germans attacked Norway on April 9, 1940, she was 31 years old, unmarried, and living in Oslo.

For many years, Sigrid Heide had run a tobacco shop in the city. She also designed and produced items made of gilt leather. Her dream, however, was to become a painter, and at the outbreak of the war, she was taking courses in drawing.

In the summer of 1941, Hitler attacked the Soviet Union. That became the signal for young Norwegian radicals to take an active part in the resistance against the Germans in Norway. Sigrid Heide joined one of the resistance groups and became a courier. She carried illegal material to people throughout Oslo and its environs, constantly risking capture by the authorities or risking betrayal by anyone who might be caught by the Germans and pressed to reveal the names of others.

That is just what happened. Sigrid Heide was betrayed. She was captured by the Gestapo on a Sunday afternoon near the end of the 1942-43 winter. The German security police had beaten the man who betrayed her so severely that he finally revealed her courier name, Markus. Until the moment of her capture, the Gestapo had thought they were searching for a man and were quite to surprised to discover that Markus was a woman.

Sigrid Heide was held alternately in the prisoners' camp at Grini or in the basement at the Gestapo prison located at Mollergarten 19 in Oslo. Though repeatedly interrogated, terrorized, and tortured, she revealed nothing.

Later, Sigrid Heide was transferred to a concentration camp in Germany northeast of Berlin. Eventually, in a group of two thousand prisoners, Sigrid Heide and sixteen or seventeen other Norwegian women were transferred to another concentration camp--Mauthausen, in Austria.

When Sigrid Heide was finally free, she told about the horror and torture she had endured, but no one believed her. Many, including her friends in Norway, laughed, saying those things could not possibly be true.

In 1946, Sigrid Heide compiled her experiences at the hands of the Germans into a book, *Kanskje i morgen--*. Though autobiographical, the book tells of the experiences of a woman named Tora. In reality, Tora was Sigrid Heide.

After her return to freedom and even after her book was published, Sigrid Heide's life was difficult. She had no real home. She tried a variety of unsuccessful jobs. After a while, she managed to further her education and worked for many years as a social worker and a consultant and adviser for disabled people.

Sigrid Heide has never married or had children, but she has had many close friends. Today, she is an elderly woman living in Oslo. Not well, she still suffers from the injuries she sustained while being tortured during the war, in the hands of her enemy.

Kanskje i morgen-- was republished in 1995 in Norway. Ethel Keshner, a retired social worker in New York City, became aware of the book and arranged its translation into English. It was from Ethel Keshner that Southfarm Press learned about Sigrid Heide, her book, and her wartime experiences.

One

"Dronningens gate!" The conductor's voice was tired, grey. Tora looked at his face, her mind at the same time on the landlady's remarks about the milk bill. She remembered the conductor from earlier days; but then his expression had not been one of resignation, nor had there been those hard lines around the mouth. The milk bill for the month had amounted to quite a bit. Could it possibly be the shortage of milk, or the complete lack of butter that had brought about this change in him--or was it all the other? All the "other." It was this that was the hardest to bear.

An errand girl with flowers eased her way cautiously further down the car. Tora smiled. She had already seen flowers that day, the first for many months. Velvety moss green drapery behind plate glass, and tulips in a dark urn. Deep red, glossy black. The sight was so unfamiliar that she stood gazing a little longer than necessary, and so beautiful that she longed to see it in the setting of her own room; but the price curbed her longing: the vase she could have for a hundred and ten, and only four kroner each for the tulips.

She sighed and her glance wandered from the errand girl to the man sitting in the innermost corner.

There was something about him she did not like. He was sitting and staring at her, but whenever she tried to catch his eye he shifted his gaze to the briefcase on her lap. This she did not like either. She was convinced that she had seen him before, but could not recall where or when. Could it be possible that he...? No--he had boarded the tram a couple of stops after her. She put the thought from her mind. But where had she seen him? He had been dressed differently then. That at least she was certain of. He'd been wearing--now he was smiling--something white. The pharmacy at Skillebekk--the assistant.

"Østbanen!" As she alighted, Tora turned at the exit and smiled broadly at him, the man who was simply the assistant at the pharmacy. He looked back at her in surprise.

She stood at the tram stop and followed the big hand of the station clock as it made its small jerks on to the next black stroke. There was the usual Saturday traffic on Jernbanetorget. Five past twelve. This part of town was not as ugly as it was reputed to be. The freezing fog in the air softened the outlines of the buildings. Six minutes past. A study in grey. Perhaps it was the tranquility of the subdued shading that made her feel that it was quite pleasant down there today. But the snow was unpleasant. Her feet were frozen. Seven past. She looked forward to a comfortable evening at home. She opened her briefcase and carefully felt the package containing her meat ration and, remembering the delicious smell of sausages at Jensen's, anticipated the evening's feast. Two ounces of sausage. Providing she didn't have to work. Why can't they be punctual? Eight past. Think if something happened, right now.

At last--Erik swung round the corner from Tomtegaten.

She noticed how he slouched; he was no more than a lad but looked washed out and unhealthy.

"Hello there!" She smiled at him.

"Police!" He hissed through his teeth, almost inaudibly, but it was too late.

Three men in civilian clothes closed in on him. Three revolvers were aimed directly at her, steadily and firmly. She looked at the man standing nearest to her. A handsome fellow, tall, dark, brown suit, beautiful hat, but with a dirty shirt. A voice whispered inside her, "Keep calm, keep calm."

"What on earth's the meaning of all this?" She heard the sound of her own voice with surprise. It was cold and steady. The man in the brown suit glared at her and took her briefcase and handbag.

"You'll find out soon enough when we get to Victoria Terrasse. We're from the German Security Forces." He continued in an odd tone: "Well, well, so this is Markus?"

She looked at him, astonished, not understanding. How could they have discovered the code name? The revolver was pressing uncomfortably against her ribs.

"You'd better come along quietly or you'll be shot!"

What a stupid thing to say, she thought--three revolvers and three grown men.... She followed without protest. She felt the continual pressure of the revolver in her side--not much, just enough.

Erik would not look at her.

A car door was opened and she was pushed into the far corner of the back seat. Erik was beside her, with one of the Gestapo in a grey greatcoat on the far side. He had not spoken a word. Tora disliked the strange look in his dark, piercing eyes. On drugs, maybe?

The man in dark blue sat at the wheel. She had not seen his face, but his back and neck emanated some feeling of decency.

The car swung up Karl Johan's gate and stopped at a red light on Stortorget.

Tora tried in vain to catch Erik's eye. He would not look at her, or did not dare to. His face was ashen. What had they done to him?

The fool--why won't he look at her? At least then he would know that she felt no animosity towards him, even though she could not understand why on earth he had not chosen Vestbanen, Sjømannsskolen or Stortorget as a meeting place; he could have asked them to turn up anywhere, just not at that place.

An Ullevål Hageby tram ground past, up Rosenkrantsgaten. Once again the car had to stop abruptly. The good looker in brown was searching the briefcase and, with a triumphant smile, pulled out the letters.

Gently, Tora, gently now, he's watching you in the rearview mirror.

"A good catch eh?" The one in the grey coat spoke in German, his ugly, harsh voice matching his cruel eyes.

"Yes, here's something to go on with." Leif's copies of the day's front line reports from London were handed over with an oily grimace.

How beautiful it is on Karl Johan today! The one in the grey coat would be sure to shoot before she managed to get the door open. People hurried by. If they only knew!

When will she walk along this street again? Maybe never. Whom have they taken already? How much do they know? Madness that they never came to any agreement on what to say in a situation like this.

The car drew to a halt in front of Victoria Terrasse. If only somebody I know would pass by at this very moment. Oh God, help me!

Two

So this is what they look like, the notorious cells at The Terrace. Whitewashed walls covered with names and dates, scratched in with--scratched in with what? A matchstick? No. A hair clip? Yes, that would do it. What's that up there? Tora stood on her toes, and spelled out the words: "Hell-- confess-- they torture to death." She moaned. She'd heard it before, she knew it was the truth; but it was so hard to have to acknowledge the truth.

"Jacob died, 7.12." Who was Jacob? How did he die?

There wasn't a single hiding place for the papers she had concealed at her breast.

"Hagen." Just the name, no date. "Hagen." He must have been interrogated here.

Perhaps the name was written just before he was shot. Had he already, even as he was scratching out his name, some premonition of what was to come? What of his poor wife and children? Even if he had not thought about death--not that kind of death--what would his thoughts have been during those last hours? She had often tried to imagine such a situation, long before she had ever become involved in the work.

She paused for a moment, reflecting over her confidence and faith, grateful for the inner security. She drifted aimlessly along the walls, recalling the words: "What shall it profit a man, if he shall gain the whole world...." Øverland's poem: "You must not slumber." This is how it must be said, this is the intensity with which it must be felt. In God's name, why can't people wake up, why can't they feel for and suffer for each other?

What was that table doing there? It was more like a trolley. The news reports! Tora turned her back to the spy hole in the door and felt the wad of papers; it was useless to think of chewing it up. What about hiding it underneath the table? She had nothing with which to fasten it--one should always carry some thumb tacks. Could they be stupid enough to allow people to go to the WC? She hammered on the door with her fist. Someone had burnt some papers over there in the corner. If only she had some matches! There was no response, so she pulled off a shoe and battered the door once more. There must be a guard somewhere. She heard the familiar thud of army boots on stone. "WC?"

"Huh?" So they say that in Germany too--the grunt had an almost homely ring to it.

"Here, quick," the guard said, probably breaking the rules.

Thank God, that's got rid of it. He had not looked through the hole.

Tora went back to her pacing. Her thoughts turned to her parents, to their feelings when the news reached them. Would it be difficult for them to understand? Perhaps even as difficult as it had been for that friend, the one who had imagined that she enjoyed the excitement of the work! He had warned her of what she was letting herself in for, begged her to think of her family and of the anguish she would bring upon them if she should be imprisoned. It was just as well that not everybody thought that way: who would do the work then?

Excitement? No--only a gradual draining of all strength. But it had not been a difficult choice. "Love thy neighbor...." One's native land, wasn't that the same as one's neighbor? This was her reason for becoming involved in the work.

How long were they going to keep her in this cell? What should she say when she was brought in for interrogation? No --it was a foolish waste of effort to attempt to work out anything, with no possible idea of what she might be asked.

Tora was suddenly overcome with fatigue and lay on her back on the table. She had breakfasted on two dry slices of bread, and it was now three o'clock. The silence was suddenly broken by the sound of wailing nearby. God, it can't be true-- they can't be doing this! She stood at the door listening, tense, her heart hammering. Was it Erik? It was not possible to recognize the voice. Someone walked past the cell, came back and stood looking through the hole. She moved a few paces and the flap fell into place.

Now the cry was no longer a shriek or a scream, but an animal howl. Almighty God, help him! She was chilled to the bone. Whistle--"Ja, vi elsker"--loudly.... There might be prisoners in the neighboring cells. If they can only keep their mouths shut, not panic and let something slip, so that others end up in this hell. She read the writing on the wall once more: "Hell--confess--they torture to death." Slowly she scratched out the last four words.

The howls subsided to a low moan.

Before the word "confess" she scratched "do not" in large letters. Her hand trembled nervously and she was bathed in a cold sweat. She was reminded of her first experience of war-- except that there had been no war here at the time. It had merely been an air raid practice.

Why didn't they fetch her for questioning? She lay down

once more. Suddenly there was a sound of footsteps and rattling keys. Someone struggled to open up. It couldn't be the guard; he would have found the correct key at once. It was the man in brown. Tora swung her legs down from the table and looked at him questioningly. "Lying down, I see. I hope you've slept well?"

She looked at his grubby collar. "Remarkably well, thank you." She had the feeling that this monster knew something about the screams. He took her upstairs.

Five men. The two new ones were a pale, slight twenty-year-old of the usual young collaborator type and a well-built German, impeccably dressed in civilian clothes. His face was hard though not entirely hostile. The contents of her handbag and briefcase lay strewn over the writing table. The twelve packets of cigarettes were neatly stacked. She realized with horror that one pack was marked with Leif's code name.

"May I have a cigarette?"

"No, they don't belong to you."

She wondered when they had started to be so scrupulous about private property.

"Name?"

"Tora Halle."

"Date of birth?"

"Eighteenth of June, nineteen hundred and nine."

What in heaven's name was that lying on top of the slices of sausage, the precious sausage which was to have been the highlight of the evening? It looked suspiciously like the two notes she sent to Leif.

"Place?"

"Skien."

"Parents living?"

"Yes."

She must see those notes.

"Address?"

"Storgaten 10, Skien."

She leaned forward quickly and snatched some slices of sausage. The men jumped instinctively. She chewed vigorously and, smiling diffidently at the one with the agreeable face, said that she had eaten only two slices of bread that day. A revolver was placed on the table.

The notes were hers. Why hadn't Leif destroyed them? Had he been caught?

"Your address here?"

"Skillebekk 7."

The man in brown studied her identity card.

"This ties up; they knew her in Skien," he said to the pale weed with the cruel eyes. She had already worked this out and was glad that she had not tried to bluff. She shivered and thrust her hand into her pocket. Good God--how could she have been so thoughtless! How many were there? Cautiously, she rolled the four local line train tickets into a hard pellet, knowing how dangerous they could be.

The one in brown launched into what seemed to be an opening speech, asking her if she was aware that this was a police interrogation and that she was duty-bound to tell the truth. She resisted the temptation to spit back that the man was a crook and that her only duty was to keep silent about the others. The man had atrocious taste in shirts--and it was crumpled.

Her mind was in a turmoil. How much did they know? What should she say? She seemed to be in a whirlpool from which there was no escape.

A part of her mind focused on things around her. The one dressed in blue paced to and fro, rattling a bunch of keys in his pocket, and she saw that the others were stationed so that there was no chance of getting rid of the paper ball. She was aware of all the sounds from outside. Strident voices from an inner office. This one in brown--there's not a trace of wisdom about him, he's not even intelligent, but doubtless cunning in a smooth way.

"Everything is cleared up," he said. "You were the only one missing. All we need to know at the moment is how long you have been involved in this work, who it was who got you into it, and the names of your subsequent contacts." He continued in a self-righteous tone: "If you tell us the truth, I can guarantee that you will be well treated and that your sentence will be light. If you refuse to cooperate, you will soon discover that we have efficient methods to force you to confess. Now be sensible, Frøken Halle. Tell us what you know and save yourself a lot of pain."

"So it is true then, people are tortured here?"

"What d'you mean?"

"You spoke about ways of forcing people to confess."

"But who says that we use torture?"

"What was that going on in the basement?"

"Nobody has said that we are going to torture you. Just tell us what you know."

She looked at him.

"I thought you said the matter was cleared up?"

"Frøken Halle, be reasonable. You are dealing with the highest German police authority. Perhaps it will help you to know that Simonson has been arrested. So have all the others you have been connected with. There are just one or two details we need you to confirm."

She did not believe him, but replied in a compliant tone:

"Very well, I am reasonable--go ahead. There's just one

thing though: who is Simonsen?"

"You don't know Simonsen?"

"I've never heard the name before--not in this connection."

"And you're a Communist?"

"No."

The four onlookers exchanged suggestive glances and shrugged resignedly.

Suddenly, the one dressed in brown hammered violently with his firsts on the table. Tora glanced across at this former charmer; his veneer had totally disappeared. "You're lying. Here you are, working with a group of dangerous Communists; you've even been in close touch with the leaders, and yet you dare to deny that you yourself are a Communist. Oh no, Frøken Halle--if you think we are fools, then you're very much mistaken."

"Can you prove that I'm a Communist?"

"Silence!" the one in grey shouted. "We're the ones who ask the questions here." The atmosphere was becoming threatening. "There's hardly any point in going on if you already think I'm lying." Her voice was sufficiently convincing so that even the man in grey appeared to relax.

"Very well--start talking."

So Tora talked.

She reflected on how incredibly easy it was to lie with a clear conscience as she followed the changing expressions of the men in the room. The one in blue was convinced and clearly believed her, until she began to speak of the second unknown person, when an expression of doubt crossed his face, but quickly changed to a smile of satisfaction as she eluded the first trap set for her by the man in brown. He suddenly broke into her story by asking:

"I assume that the tokens you write about here refer to the ten thousand kroner?"He waved the note to Leif in her face.

Ah, you old fox, you thought you were smart there, but you weren't. Marit, how could you know what an angel you were when you gave me these this morning. Tora pulled two bread vouchers from her pocket and placed them in front of him on the desk.

"No, this is what I was referring to."

He made no attempt to disguise his disappointment. "Do you have any other papers on you?" She made no resistance to his search, but shuddered with repulsion as his hands passed over her. It had taken some time for him to hit on this idea. He was relishing it too. Loathsome--but it gave her some time to sort out her confused ideas. One thing was certain, they knew that she had collected the money, but they did not know where she had fetched it, nor from whom. Who could possibly have told them in the first place? Leif or Erik? Or Sørholt? They said that Erik had told them that he got it from her, but had given it back on the following day. That was true. She wondered how much they had tortured him. It was good that he knew no more than he did. Contacts were vital and must be kept secret at all costs. She had to take that chance with the money--in any case, they've stolen enough from this country. She noticed that they were not troubling to examine the back of her body as intimately as the front. Simonsen--so that was Leif's real name. That was all they knew, so far.

It was five o'clock. How long would they keep this up? Her fingerprints had been taken, and a sample of her handwriting. There was no chance of succeeding with any deception here. Why didn't you destroy the notes, Leif?

She was asked the same questions, over and over again, but remembered what she had said; there was no change. Just as she was thinking that they had at last finished with her, the one in grey suddenly barked: "Bring him in!"

Two Gestapo emerged from the inner office with Sørholt between them.

He too....

He stood there, erect and with an expression of intransigence. His hands were tied behind his back and his figure seemed to exude an air of detached scorn.

As he was being led away, she said quickly, and so loudly that he was bound to hear: "I've only seen him once--and I don't know his name."

She immediately wondered if she had made a mistake; but they had both the letter to Leif and to him, so they would never have believed her if she had denied everything.

A barrage of questions followed. "So he was the one who had fetched the money?"

"No!" "Where had she seen him?" "Østbanen." "Whom had he been talking to?" "Leif." This was a connection they already knew about. She had not spoken to him. She had no idea who he was, she said. At last it was over. She was led back to the cell where she lay down on the table and closed her eyes.

How could one day be so interminable! She was exhausted beyond any ability to think. She tried to relax, to let fatigue slowly engulf her entire body, but it was impossible to rest. If only they don't manage to wear down Sørholt. If they've got Leif, why wasn't she confronted with him too? They read Randi's letter with hardly a comment. It had seemed sacrilegious at the time; but maybe they too were touched by some deep, hidden sense of integrity and truth, for she had noticed, as he read, that the one in brown had grown strangely silent and ill at ease.

He had accepted without protest, the explanation of the

photograph of Harald: a friend totally unconnected with the case. Only the grey-suited one protested, angrily demanding a name and address, but seemed satisfied when she had asked him if he seriously imagined that she would have carried the photograph on her if he had been one of those involved.

Her thoughts of Harald were suddenly interrupted by the sound of rattling keys. The guard led her up to an anteroom. Sørholt was there, as erect and somber as ever. His hands were no longer tied behind his back, but he was handcuffed. She smiled faintly and was answered by a helpless movement of his hands towards his pocket. He drew out a handkerchief and wiped his mouth. It was immediately flecked with red. What have they done, have they hit him, or pulled out his teeth?

She knew that this was just the beginning.

Out and into the same car, the same seat, the same guards; only Erik was not there. She had a feeling that he was the one who had been tortured in the basement, and that they would carry on with him through the night. She found herself able to contemplate calmly the possibility that he probably would not manage to hold out. It was not to be wondered at, nor indeed worth thinking about.

An enema of boiling oil was the worst she could imagine. This she had heard of, and other refined torments: burning and the drawing of fingernails were evidently quite effective. That humans could become so brutalized....

Tora knew that in her capacity to experience a described situation as intensely as if she were living through it herself, she had a strength possessed by few others. Such an ability inevitably inflicted unnecessary pain, but she looked upon it as an advantage in the work, since it prepared her for anything which might come. Those with whom she had tried to discuss this gift had protested, had not wanted to listen or even think about it, preferring to blot out any such idea.

Sørholt was composed. It was so dark in the car that she dared to stroke his hands. He asked the Gestapo to loosen the handcuffs slightly since they were cutting into his flesh, but his request was only answered by a harsh laugh.

Three

The car pulled up before a large dark building. It must be Grini.

In a second floor office, there were German guards and men in drab prison garb in full activity.

The overriding impression was of uproar. Not one instruction was given in a normal voice, but everything was shouted in German. The prisoners resembled automatons, their faces expressionless. Doors were left open and the tumult continued, with the sound of stamping boots and jangling keys everywhere.

Personal details were noted on file cards and watches and jewelry confiscated and placed in sealed envelopes. Sørholt's mouth was still bleeding but even the prisoners did not appear to notice. When they had finished with him he was led away.

A grandmotherly, grey-haired woman with a bunch of keys on a cord around her waist appeared and led Tora to the women's section. Momentarily forgetting that she was a prisoner, Tora stepped aside to allow the older woman to pass first through the door. She was immediately rewarded with a sharp blow with the keys; but in the stairway to the third floor it was explained that prisoners must always walk ahead of the guards. No more was said, but Tora had the feeling that the old woman was appraising her and that she was not entirely unfriendly.

They entered another office, this time with a more feminine appearance; but the new guard appeared to be made of steel and spoke with a harsh, peremptory tone. "Off with your clothes!" Every garment was closely examined. Tora looked at her extraordinary face, noting the strange, feline quality of the eyes. She would have been attractive if she had only smiled. Surely it must be possible to thaw this frozen exterior?

Tora struggled with a sensation of being rendered powerless by the hard face.

In a normal, courteous voice Tora asked the woman what her name was, but it was obvious from the expression on her face that any such familiarity was forbidden. A look of longing to hit Tora passed across her face, but she controlled herself and replied brusquely: "Prisoners are not permitted to ask such questions."

The Grandmother reappeared. She looked questioningly at the guard as Tora dressed, eliciting a testy reply: "Nothing, absolutely nothing!"

"I told you that all this was totally unnecessary. I have no papers on me. And besides, I've already been searched once before." Tora carefully pulled on her threadbare, woolen stockings, realizing that they would not last for many more days. The tigress bared her teeth and snarled something in incomprehensible German.

Tora straightened up, and looking calmly at the warder, told her that in Norway only animals were muzzled; human beings were free to express themselves--even prisoners. Tora saw a flash of yellow in the woman's eyes and she reminded Tora again of a tigress poised to spring. The Grandmother remained a silent witness, although there was a faint glimmer of amusement in her expression as she hustled the prisoner from the room, mumbling something about insolence. Tora understood that this was intended more to mollify the tigress than as a reprimand to Tora.

They walked along a long corridor. Tora sensed an aura of suffering. It seemed to drift with such intensity from some of the cells that she could hardly refrain from weeping; behind those doors, all was silent, but behind others she could hear murmuring and occasionally loud talking. Every sound was audible. Somewhere several people seemed to be marching back and forth, singing a patriotic song in harmony; a strong contralto drowned the two sopranos. The Grandmother struck the door with her keys and the singing stopped, but the footsteps continued, louder and firmer than before.

The old woman unlocked a ground floor cell, adjacent to the entrance to the men's section. She hesitated in the doorway and spoke, advising Tora to adopt Olga's sensible attitude in all things; then shaking her head, she slammed the door behind her.

Tora introduced herself to the two occupants and was told that their names were Olga and Signe. Signe was slightly built, thin and dejected, with poor hearing, so that Olga answered the questions of the newcomer.

"Sh!--we must be quiet," she said. "Someone could be standing outside listening."

"But we must be allowed to talk?"

A faint smile passed over her wan face.

"Yes, but it doesn't always pay--and anyway, we don't always feel like talking."

"No, of course not." Feeling uncertain, Tora withdrew. She wandered about the cell, turning the remarks over in her mind. Doesn't always pay? Why wouldn't they talk to her?

"You'll understand better when you've been sitting here

for eight months like us," Olga suddenly explained. Tora only nodded and kept on walking, feeling there was much that she already understood. One, two, three, four, five, turn. She doesn't want to become like them. Olga would probably have been good-looking if it were not for that unhealthy fat and prison-grey pallor. One, two, three, four, five, turn. Why is Signe so dejected? Is it inevitable that one should end up with that look of resignation and indifference? One, two, three--I will not--I will not--dear God, spare me from such apathy!

The cell was furnished with an unpainted table in front of the window, two narrow bunkbeds along one wall, with a third bed opposite a small cupboard. A malodorous zinc bucket stood under the sink.

"What exactly do you do here all day?"

"If you'll just sit down, I'll tell you. It's so distracting when you keep wandering up and down like that."

Fair enough--so now she knew. Tora sat down on the bed.

"I'll tell you what we do, we sit." "All day long?" "Yes, except when we're taken out for an airing." "An airing?" "Yes, if it's fine we're taken out into the compound for about fifteen minutes." "But there must be some kind of work?" "We darn the male prisoners' socks. You'll get to like that." "What kind of books are you allowed to read?" "You a bit slow on the uptake or something? This isn't a hotel you've come to."

Olga shouted to Signe, "She's asking what kind of books we get!"

They were both silently amused and Tora was embarrassed by her own gullibility.

The two women began to undress. They washed hastily in the water which had been standing in the sink, and lay down. It was evident that the upper bunk was hers. Tora wondered what to do, with no soap, no washcloth, no toothbrush. She undressed and stood in front of the sink, contemplating the ring of grease around the edge. She shuddered, and remembering the pimpled back of one of the other women, gave up the idea of using the sink that evening.

She gave her face and arms a hurried splash in the cold running water, and brushed it off with her hands as best she could. She had so far been given no towel.

"Shall I turn out the light and open the window?" Olga answered dryly that the light switch was in the corridor and that Signe's ears were so painful that she could not bear to have the window open. The mattress was nothing but a mass of hard lumps. However, the bedclothes were clean and Tora was glad to lie down. But the air was foul and the cell was filled with a strange smell of something sickly, something greyish-brown and slimy. It was impossible to sleep.

Someone drew aside the metal flap over the spy hole and looked in. The light was switched off but there was no peace. There was a constant opening and closing of doors. The metallic rattling of keys was the worst.

There was a sudden sound of hammering on the door to the men's unit. It became louder and louder. The quick, light footsteps of a woman were heard in the corridor. A door was unlocked and the sound of a berating man's voice was interrupted by the deep voice of a woman. The heavy tread of two men then sounded in the corridor, together with the light click of high heels. Yet another door was opened and an order given. Mumbling voices and wild sobs sounded in the passage. The sobs grew louder and louder. It sounded as though somebody had stumbled immediately outside the cell and brutal shouts were heard:

"Bloody swine, don't be such an idiot!" Shortly afterwards a car drew up outside. Voices and the rattling of swords were followed by the slamming of a car door. Then silence.

Tora was aware that the whole building was listening, every nerve alert and tense. Her heart was hammering painfully.

The memory of the strain of the afternoon's interrogation welled up in her. Maybe it will be her turn next. How much do they know? Who has been caught? What have they said? They torture women too, that she knows.

All at once a strange feeling of confidence blotted out her fears. She was not worried for herself, but wondered where they had taken the prisoner. For questioning at The Terrace or else? Merciful God, give him strength.

What was that noise? Where was she?

Tora sat up in bed, suddenly wide awake.

Grini. Questioning. What do they know? No, this endless speculation, this pointless dread of what was to come, she must stop it.

There was a din of keys, doors and buckets from the passage. Olga turned in her bed. Tora looked down at her and, seeing that she was awake, asked her what all the commotion was about.

"Latrine drill. It's our turn soon so you'd better get dressed and be ready."

Tora felt that it was hopeless to attempt to wash without a cloth, and hoped that she would eventually be given a towel. She dried herself with her slip and looked about for a mirror and comb. Olga sat on the edge of her bed and followed the movements of the new prisoner with a desultory gaze.

"If you're looking for a mirror, we use that." She pointed to the lid of the latrine bucket.

"I haven't got a comb either."

"Use mine, it's lying on the sink."

Tora looked at her gratefully. She gave her lifeless, greasy hair a quick glance; no doubt she had dandruff too. Tora gave the comb a surreptitious wipe, shuddering at such filth, and bent reluctantly to look in the "mirror." She recoiled in disgust.

"The sooner you drop your fancy ways in here the better," Olga remarked, with a wide and unexpectedly sweet smile.

The noise in the passage was getting nearer. "Just follow me, I can hear it's Funcke today," Olga whispered. She grabbed the bucket and dashed out as the door opened. The tigress from yesterday was standing outside.

"Now then--at the double!" The command was like the crack of a whip.

It was no wonder that Olga ran. To have chased after her would have been the line of least resistance; but Tora forced herself to walk down the passage at a normal pace. "Get a move on! Quicker! she heard behind her as she followed Olga through the door.

"You looked so comical, tearing along with that bucket," she said to Olga, laughing. A three-quarter high partition separated the cubicles.

"Sh! She's in a bad mood today. You must hurry." Olga left. Tora took her time. She had made up her mind that she was not going to chase about like a scared rabbit for these warders.

So Funcke is her name. Her stocky frame positively quivered with authority and suppressed impatience as she stood waiting. The memory of an old picture of an angel, standing with drawn sword at the entrance to the Garden of Eden, suddenly passed through Tora's mind. The militant angel resembled the personification of eternal peace compared with Funcke. Tora smiled at her as she passed, willing the woman to reveal herself as human just one time, but was met with a look that would kill, a murderous, sullen glower.

Breakfast consisted of four thin slices of dry bread and a cup
of ersatz coffee. Tora was never hungry at that early hour; she
was satisfied with two slices and was surprised to hear that her
fellow prisoners could have easily devoured three times the
ration. They immediately began to discuss the midday meal
but, tiring of all the talk of food, Tora tried to steer the conversation in a different direction. She launched into an im-
passioned tirade, airing in violent terms her hatred of the Nazi
regime and dismay at those who were still so cautious, always
hedging their bets, not sure of who was going to win the war.
Signe and Olga grew silent and withdrawn. They showed no
interest whatsoever in Tora's warnings that people should stop
being so selfish, wake up and accept their share of the blame for
the tragedy of the war. She was at a loss to understand their
apathy, feeling as she did that she would never be able to come
to terms with her own guilt for shirking her duty to her
country.

Politics was rotten--corrupt through and through. They
were all feathering their own nests as best they could. Self-
interest and lust for power were the driving forces behind
everything. Damn those men who had brought about this hell
on earth! This had been her sole line of thought until she had
suddenly become aware of her own responsibility. She was still
tormented by the memory of her own apathy and indifference; but at least now she had tried to repent through using
her life where the need was greatest, in the struggle for
freedom.

It was terrible that it should all have ended in this way. She
had desperately wanted to carry on the work in the world
outside; but it was a consolation to know that even in captivity

something could be achieved: by keeping quiet she could enable others out there to carry on and, through endurance, endeavor to show that there were those who could not be intimidated by force.

She suddenly realized that it was Sunday and asked if any services were held. They smiled and told her that the only change in the usual routine was the after dinner rest, and that the prisoners were not exercised on that day. The other two were in a more communicative mood, so she got to know more. Olga was married and had a three-year-old son. Poor thing! She must be thinking of the child when she sat for so long, oblivious to her surroundings.

Tora tried to imagine how it would be to be a mother, shut up inside here, and dreamed of the child she had never had.

Olga brought her back from her reverie by telling her the secret of survival in prison:

"Just take it easy--see that you don't rub them the wrong way."

Well, that was certainly one way of getting by--sensible, no doubt; but Tora was not convinced that it was always right to be so unquestioningly sensible. Time would tell. At least she now understood the meaning behind what the Grandmother had said to her as she had let her into the cell.

She learned that the director of the women's unit was Frøken Freyer, and that the old warder who had shown her in was simply known as Grandma. Signe loosened up too; she talked about her sweetheart who had been sent with the first shipment of prisoners to Germany, and of her seventy-year-old father, who was also at Grini. It was no longer difficult to understand her misery, nor the silence which followed, and it was a relief when it was broken by the arrival of food.

Dinner consisted of a bowl of soup--"storm soup" the others call it. A grey-green, unappetizing slop of potatoes. But small globules of fat floated on the surface, and after her diet outside of little else but turnips, dried fish and black herring cakes, the soup tasted good.

The following afternoon she was fetched by Grandma. "Take your belongings with you!" she said brusquely. Tora looked questioningly at Olga. What could this mean? Her cellmates stood to attention beside their stools, their faces expressionless. She turned to Grandma, who waited in the doorway, cold and unapproachable.

"Quickly! Take everything with you. Understand?"

Tora noticed a slight difference in the woman's tone of voice and manner. This is the moment when she should pull herself up, click her heels and say: "Jawohl!" She answered with an inaudible "yes" and took down her hat and coat. Her gloves had already been taken from her. Belongings? She had none. Only the towel she had been given that day and a strip of canvas Signe had given her. It had been used to clean the sink and was stiff and grey and slimy when wet. She took it with her, and barely managed to glance at Olga and Signe before she was pushed out and the door to the cell locked.

It was strange to leave them and she had a premonition that a bad time lay ahead. The Gestapo have probably discovered that her statement was nothing but "invention and damned lies." But if that were so, who could have told them? Have they uncovered more? Where have things started to unravel? They may have discovered the money as well. Surely she doesn't need the towel in an interrogation? Perhaps she is going to be moved to a single cell? She turned to Grandma and asked her where they were going. "Go on--quickly!" The woman poked her in the back with a key. It reminded her of

a revolver. They stopped outside a door at the far end of the
passage.

So, she was on her own. Was this where the torment
began? She squared her shoulders a little. She had a suspicion
that Grandma was standing outside and spying on her. Perhaps
they look to see how new prisoners react to being alone. She
took off her shoes, moved the pillow so that she could lie with
her face toward the door, and lay down. Her suspicion was
correct, and the door was immediately opened. Grandma's
grey locks shook with anger and she pointed a warning finger
at the sinner, who lay staring at her.

"Get up! That's forbidden, strictly forbidden!"

"Why? I'm tired." Tora sat up and looked at her with
surprise. It was quite amusing to observe the changing e-
motions mirrored in her face; she seemed unable to make up
her mind. Was the prisoner insolent, or did she simply not
understand that she was in a German prison? Was she stupid or
totally innocent? Her expression changed from anger to tolerance. She pointed to her wristwatch. "Six. After supper--not
before!" Tora began to tie her shoelaces and Grandma left.

This cell was the same size as the other one but the table was
placed against the long wall. Six steps from the window to the
door instead of five as before. Not much exercise to be had
here. If she took small steps and walked round the room, then
there would be thirteen paces, but there was far too little room
to get up any speed. She drifted slowly round with her hands
behind her back, whistling. She had a feeling that she was
being observed. The metal flap over the spy hole was in place,
but in the center there was a small hole, the size of a pinhead.
From inside the cell it resembled no more than a black dot, and
it was not possible to see if it were being used. There were

many strange sounds in the passage, footsteps coming from she knew not where, nor where they ended. She was convinced now that she was being watched.

Tora stood in front of the window. An angry rattling of keys confirmed her suspicion that she was being watched. Judging from the impatient jangling it must be Funcke. "What are you doing over there?" It was Funcke. Tora half turned from the window. "What am I doing? Looking out of the window!" She fell for it: "Ah, my child, that is forbidden, strictly forbidden!" The simple tactic had worked: the woman's tone was milder already. "Why is that?" Funcke replied in what was for her the simplest way: she left, just as swiftly and impatiently as she had arrived. "Children can be so guileless, and their foolish questions so irritating." A faint smile crossed Tora's face.

When would the next interrogation be? It was as though she stood at the edge of a deep abyss, waiting for an avalanche to engulf her. She felt it coming, nearer and nearer. She waited.

The so-called evening round was beginning. Each cell was allocated a bucket of hot water which the prisoners fetched themselves. The noise grew nearer, travelling along the passage; but no one opened up for her. There was a kind of water closet connected to the sink in the cell; but surely she was to have hot water and food?

All was quiet for a while when she suddenly recognized the same sound of high-heeled shoes as she had heard the previous night. They stopped outside her cell and the door was unlocked. "Here's your meal." It was Freyer's flat, impassive voice. The image of a plucked fledgling passed through Tora's mind. Freyer was thin and sallow with dark hair scraped back

into a tight knot in the nape of her neck. An air of outer indifference and inner helplessness emanated from her slight
figure. In that brief moment it was impossible for the prisoner
to gain any impression of the eyes behind the spectacles.
Freyer wished her goodnight as she locked the door. Tora was
so overcome that she forgot to ask for water.

The days passed uneventfully. Tora was alone with the
advancing avalanche. Always alone. The weather was fine.
Every morning the others went out for exercise but not she.
Occasionally she heard the prisoners laughing and talking as
they walked along the passage. It sounded as though the inmates of the cell opposite were enjoying themselves: they sang
and talked and laughed all day long. She was so alone. When
she asked Funcke why she was never taken out, the reply was
always the same: "Later!" followed by the slam of the door. She
had asked for a comb and toothbrush on several occasions.
The reply was always the same: "Wait," or "Later." She grew
to hate the words. The warders had much to do and
presumably forgot, but she felt that it was unfair. If they only
knew how it was to have long, uncombed hair, and no
toothbrush. She felt as though her mouth were slowly
clogging up. If she could only get hold of a cigarette! She
became restless, unable to sleep, and the thought of cigarettes
haunted her all day--interrogation and cigarettes. Why can't
they begin and let her get finished with it? The waiting was
driving her insane. She was lonely and longed to have
someone to talk to. Grandma and Funcke never had time and
frequently slammed the door as she was in mid-sentence. It felt
like a blow, a sharp stabbing at her heart, every time the door
clanged to. She wanted to cry, to throw herself on her bed and
drown in uncontrolled sobbing.

Two new guards appeared. One was immensely tall and quite attractive, but her smile was spiteful. She never replied when spoken to but merely smiled her hateful smile and slammed the door, seeming to enjoy the act. She appeared once or twice during the evening washing. Tora was unable to bear her repugnant smile on those occasions, shuddering at the slimy smile which seemed to still hang in the air after she was gone. Funcke was different: evil, but with a certain cleanness nonetheless.

The other new one was worse. A vast, shapeless mass, totally lacking in any ability to understand. She was huge, her bulk unnerving. Her skin and complexion were good and her hair dark and curly. The large, round eyes had an expression of childish curiosity. Her massive arms and hands resembled gigantic, fleshy clubs, and her thighs those of a powerful drayhorse. Tora retreated instinctively to the far wall when she came in. Her crude strength seemed to pervade the entire cell and there was room for none other.

Tora did not collapse onto her bed in tears: she walked up and down, whistling and thinking about the words "Love thy neighbor. Love thine enemy. Do unto others as you would be done by." Dear Lord, you must help me--I need more guidance. There's nothing about if your enemy is like this or like that. Nothing more than simply "Love thine enemy" and "Do unto others as you would be done by."

When they came in the evening to put out the lights, she would lie with childishly folded hands on the blanket, feigning sleep. She knew that they were looking at her. Frequently. Often for long periods. A foolish demonstration she would have thought, in other circumstances: now she wants them to know the reason why she doesn't seize the chair and hurl it at her captor, why she doesn't protest when they are inhumanly cruel, why she doesn't strike when the tall one smiles her slimy smile. She wants them to understand the reason why she is not filled with hate.

Four

Tora was awakened by incoherent bellowing from the parade ground in front of the building. Hoarse commands were being shouted. What was going on? She went to the window.

The entire square was lit up. The sentries were marching at regulation pace before the entrance gates. It was bitterly cold and their boots crunched on the snow at every step.

Why were they carrying out these exercises with prisoners in the middle of the night? Twenty men in light, summer weight prison garb, their heads bare. Their hands were tied behind their backs. Tora caught her breath--the prisoners were barefoot. She sensed how their feet stiffened in the cold, how the gravel and lumps of ice cut into the bare skin, how the wind strafed their thin bodies. The one commanding them must be quite mad. He seemed to be the devil incarnate as he sprang, with a whip in one hand and a pistol in the other. He hounded the men round and round, lashing out haphazardly. Occasionally he missed and stumbled. He was drunk.

The tempo was too slow for him. The prisoners gasped and staggered in the snow. Some fell helplessly, to be kicked into action by the shrieking drunk. One lay screaming, unable to rise. A kick, another kick and he was swept aside, silent.

Tora trembled, choking at every kick, quivering at every

39

whipstroke until, able to bear no more, she tried to turn away, but was transfixed.

The drunk grew wilder and wilder and started to sing. The prisoners were commanded to sing as they moved forward with hare-like jumps. Their desperate leaps were not good enough for the man with the whip. He kicked one over and struck another in the head with his revolver, continuously shrieking his song.

The pacing of the sentries at the gate increased in tempo. The prisoners were unable to carry on singing. Their voices broke and the strange sound became more redolent of sobbing than of song. The monster raved and screamed. One man rolled over onto his side, while the hopping of the others quickened and their singing grew louder, taking on a tone of insane fear. Several men simply screamed the words "I am a dog--of a Jewish swine--." The rest disintegrated into an indescribable, gurgling sound. At last the man with the whip was satiated. He staggered from side to side, round and round, still hoarsely screeching the refrain, over and over again. More prisoners fell, some lay motionless, others crawled away, all unnoticed. The drunken song was now no more than a babble and the gasping chorus dwindled to a moan.

Silence and an inky darkness descended on the parade ground. The madman called for light and there was a shout from the guardhouse. Tora was able to understand the words "blackout" and "air defense." The gate was opened and the unsteady footsteps and babbling voice vanished down the road.

Tora fell to the floor in front of the window. Her teeth chattered. She had come to a bottomless hell of pain. She heard a metal flap being drawn aside and saw that the light had been switched on, but she was unable to move.

Grandma came in. Tora saw that she was speaking but could not understand what she was saying. Tora did not attempt to answer or get up but only stared at the woman.

Grandma stood for a moment. There was an odd look about her. She turned in the doorway on her way out and said something in a hoarse voice which Tora was not able to understand. It was of no consequence; nothing mattered any longer. Twenty cracked prisoners' voices were tearing at her soul; she was being slowly killed by a drunken song.

"Why are you sitting there? Why aren't you dressed?" Funcke's hard voice cut through the flood of pain, which was breaking over Tora in incessant waves.

"Frøken Funcke, do you know what goes on here at night?"

"What do you mean?" The voice was tense, wary.

"Do you know what hell is?"

"The prisoner must be out of her mind? There's such an unnatural look in her eyes. The poor little thing must have something to help her sleep."

"No--I don't need anything to help me sleep. And I'm not mad--yet," Tora answered calmly, and went on to relate what she had seen.

Funcke merely replied, in a voice devoid of expression, "It isn't true;" but she forgot to add that it was against the rules to look out of the window.

"Ask the old woman, the one who was on duty." Tora began to dress and Funcke left, leaving four slices of bread on the table. She could not bear the thought of food. Air, fresh air: she longed to get out and breathe in fresh air.

She walked ceaselessly up and down, not whistling, not thinking of the approaching avalanche, not thinking about cigarettes. The others were taken out for exercise. She heard them but was not concerned. She lived with the cracked voices. There were no longer twenty, only eighteen. Tora wept and silently entreated them: "You must not allow yourselves to hate, because if you do, then you'll die." She carried on walking--back and forth, back and forth.

At about dinner time, the tall Gestapo fellow came to fetch her for questioning. As they climbed the stairs to the first floor he spoke to her. "Frøken Halle, I advise you to tell the truth. You see, we know everything so it is quite useless to come up with any more excuses."

The two she had seen before, the one in grey and the one in blue, were waiting, together with a new person in German uniform. The one in blue looked worried, while the little grey fellow paced restlessly up and down, smoking. The stranger was sitting leafing through a booklet and barely glanced up as they entered. Then he lit a cigarette and, nonchalantly crossing his legs, began to look her up and down. The cigarette smoke drifted towards the window. She turned toward the stranger and surveyed his gleaming high boots and row of medals. Then, fixing her gaze on the curious blue eyes, she quickly said: "You have taken twelve packs of cigarettes from me. May I have one of them?" He smiled, somewhat taken aback, and was about to offer her one when the little one butted in: "No, I'm damned if she shall! She's served us up a pack of lies and unless she tells us the truth pretty quickly, the only thing she's going to get is a bullet!" He seated himself at the writing table. Tora seized the edges of the table in a frenzied grip and leaned towards him, stuttering with rage and indignation. "How dare you speak to me of bullets! You should be using them on that one who was tormenting prisoners to death in the square last night. Prisoners dressed in only summer clothes

--barefoot--chained. It's inhuman!" She came to a halt for lack of words. "Norwegians are quite good at German!" The small fellow looked ironically from her to the stranger. "Yes--and hot tempered!" The stranger smiled a derisory, taunting smile; but then his expression suddenly changed, the teasing over. "Let's get to the point!"

Now the interrogation took on a different form: some questions were put in a different way, others were new. In an attempt to loosen her tongue they let out information which both confused and shocked her. There seemed to be no point except that it helped her to understand more of what they knew and did not know. Threats were no longer disguised by smooth words; she was asked outright how she would like to be tortured. Her simple answer was that since they did not believe the explanation she had already given, there was no more to say. All the threats and savagery in the world could change nothing. She was told that she would start to talk willingly soon enough--or be silenced once and for all.

Tora fixed her attention on the barracks which could be seen from the window. Male prisoners were chopping wood, shifting stones, stacking planks, or just moving about. "It's nice to see some men again," she said to the man in blue, nodding towards the window. The grey one swore. She had evidently not heard his last question. "Get her out of here! She has two hours to think things over!"

On the way down to the cell the one in brown spoke to her gravely: "Frøken Halle! I'm Norwegian. You can confide in me. I promise you, I can arrange for you to be let out soon if you will only explain the setup in a little more detail. Did you know any of the men in Drammen, for example?" She gave him a questioning look. "On that last occasion when you fetched the letter to Simonsen." What sweet satisfaction it would have given her to have replied openly: "What an utter disgrace that a man like you should go around saying he's Norwegian! Your type is the last one should confide in. Your polished courtesy and pretense of friendliness are doubly dangerous coupled with the raw brutality of the Germans. Your lies are so smooth one can almost believe them. That false, mild expression. I know it's all a sham. You should be ashamed!" How wonderful it would have been to speak out. Instead, she looked directly at him. "Do you too really believe I'm lying? I've already told you, I've never seen Drammen." Well, that was more or less true since it had always been raining and foggy or dark when she had been there.

Two hours, he'd said. Tora already felt that she had been turning things over in her mind for an eternity. As far as she was concerned the answer was simple: it would be best to confess something of what they already knew. Things had already gone to pieces in one area, so no more damage could be done there. On the other hand, she had contacts in other branches, and all those working outside were of greater use than she was now. So that was it. The afternoon passed. She waited and waited but nobody came.

Funcke offered her a sleeping tablet in the evening but she refused. She wanted to have a clear head if something happened; but nothing did happen. She lay with closed eyes, not sleeping. She could not get the tune from the previous night out of her head, and tried to think of something else. A mental vision of a bleeding toothless mouth floated before her and she heard a voice, swearing to shut her mouth once and for all. She tried to imagine what it would be like to be shot. Better than being tortured to death, no doubt. She would ask not to be blindfolded. It must be better to be able to see right to the last second--in spite of everything. She heard footsteps in the pas-

sage. Were they coming here? No. She was not afraid to die.
Quite sure? Yes, she believed in the eternal life, that this life
was just the beginning of a continual process of development.
She was not afraid of death--but that she might fail in her faith.
Her fear was not of failing in the eyes of others. All humans fail,
continually, even if they do not always understand their
weakness, or are not sufficiently honest to admit it to others
than themselves; and sometimes not even that. This was not
the fear that haunted her, but something different, something
deep inside her, something not her own but touching upon
the deep wellspring of her faith. She was frightened when she
thought about torture because she knew that if she failed on
this account, she would have betrayed her faith. But it was
because of her trust in God that she trusted her ability to endure. Others only laughed at her confidence, or were irritated
and asked how she could be so sure of herself. It was not herself
she was sure of; but they could not or would not understand, so
that it was useless to say more. And when all was said and done,
she had no actual experience of such a situation, so how could
she know? There was a jangling of keys. Were they coming
now? Not now either. Would she never get that tune out of
her head? How was the owner of the drunken voice today?
Was he tormented by a bad conscience? Does he vent his anger
on others because of this torment? Or is he no more than an
animal? A monster? No--no one is just an animal. How had he
become like that? How had he aimed his blows so that when
they struck they made that sound of splintering bone? Surely
the family must be safe when they live in a different town? If
only Marit isn't captured and prevented from carrying on. Was
it a mistake to take that chance with the money? No. Dina
would have known that something was wrong when she
hadn't called in with the news as usual. Marit must have been

worried when she hadn't turned up for coffee as arranged. She
must have rung her sister. No, she would have gone up to her.
Explained. And then they would wait for a few days. It was
terrible that they should have to endure all this anxiety for her.
Gerd has other things to occupy her mind--connected with
the work. If only she doesn't wait too long to look for the
money. She's bound to try to fetch it, even though she knows
that there will be a guard there. It would be easier for her as a
sister. Surely it must be possible to visit one's sister without
being suspected? She would manage if she were taken.
Fortunately she knows nothing. The landlady is a good sort.
She must have understood that something was going on. The
conversation was always broken off or petered out whenever
the landlady got onto the subject. She wouldn't say anything.
There's no risk of any unpleasantness either, not when she had
her own entrance. What's the time? Was there any chance of
their coming now?

Tora tried to detach herself from the never ending flow of
thought. A drunken voice reverberated in her ear. How will it
go in the morning if she can't get to sleep tonight either? Her
head felt so strange. If only she had a cigarette....

There was a banging in the passage. Was it morning already? Were they coming after all? The door was unlocked.
Her heart was thudding. It was Funcke, only Funcke, with
some slices of bread. She passed no comment on finding her
still in bed. "You must eat--it may be a long time to dinner."
What did she mean by that? Did she too know that the
avalanche was drawing nearer? Was she trying to prepare her
for the interrogation? It wasn't necessary. She was prepared.

Tora washed herself with the sticky rag. It was repulsive.
She had asked for soap again the previous day. "You'll get it on

Saturday." "A comb?" "Yes, later." Her scalp itched. She attempted to comb her hair with her fingers but this only made it more bedraggled. She ate all the bread although she was not hungry. It was tasteless but she took her time, chewing slowly. It could be a long time to dinner.

She was given water to wash the floor. Funcke said nothing, nor did the prisoner. She washed the floor thoroughly. It was good to have something to do. She stumbled as she placed the bucket outside and the warder looked at her quickly. Her expression seemed to say, the prisoner has grown so pale and the rings under her eyes grow darker every day. Why can't she confess? Then she won't have to be alone. Why do they get mixed up in these things? Why do they bother to put up a fight? They must know that we are in the right. Germany is winning on every front. Funcke could afford to smile as she closed the door with a self-satisfied clang.

Tora was tired. It would be wonderful to lie down and escape from everything in sleep. She wished that they would come so that she could get it over with.

The new warder came. "Out!" she commanded. When they were in the passage she said: "You're stupid not to confess." Tora was overcome with rage and a desire to fling herself upon this mountain of flesh. Her fatigue had vanished, anger seeming to square her shoulders and stiffen her resolve to fight.

For the Gestapo, the interrogation produced nothing new. The prisoner hardly opened her mouth. The undersized individual in grey, who was the most aggressive, quivered with anger. With two catlike leaps he was on top of her, shaking his clenched fists at her head and spitting questions into her face. She did not react, did not draw back, but calmly stood her ground and looked at him. What the devil does she think she's up to with that insolent stare? He had the urge to knock her over. This isn't the way she should be reacting: she should be angry or afraid. She's not innocent and has no business to stand there looking like a child. He could not endure that stare. But just wait....

In the afternoon she was fetched by Grandma for further questioning. "Where are we going?" Tora was afraid of The Terrace. "To Dentzer, the boss here." She reeled off a long and unintelligible title. "My child, be sensible. Just own up, then you'll be transferred to the open unit where you'll be much better off. Be sensible." Tora smiled at her. Grandma never screamed when she spoke, unlike most of the others in the place.

As soon as she saw Dentzer, she understood why she had been brought before him. Well-fed and on the whole well-proportioned, he appeared to revel both in his elegant uniform and in his own irresistibility. These Gestapo people have probably said that she needs tougher treatment. Dentzer had doubtless thought it over. Those people up at The Terrace aren't always so smart in the way they treat their prisoners. They certainly don't understand women. Send her to me first, then we'll see. He probably has it all worked out.

He had a splendid voice, but too powerful for a normal room. It was tiring to listen to him.

To begin with, his manner was mild, pleasant. Courteous, almost cultivated. Perhaps she would like an interpreter? "Yes, thank you." Grandma broke in, saying that this was not necessary. An interpreter was sent for. He was a young boy in uniform. His head seemed to be thrust far out from his body and waved from side to side as he walked. He seemed to sniff the air as if trying to pick up the scent of someone or something.

There was an office girl there also, a shapely specimen of a German street girl.

"So, to the matter in hand then." Dentzer blew smoke into the prisoner's face with an air of satisfaction. She was asked to go through her statement.

It did not take long before he broke in, first with a roar and then the thunder of clenched fists on the table. "Do you really want us to believe this tale?" "Of course!" This was indeed what she wanted--but she had little hope of their doing so. "You are an accomplished liar, young lady," he said, and leafed through some papers. He suddenly flung the papers onto the table and jumped up. "Aha! A Communist." Any pretence of courtesy was at an end. He rampaged up and down the room, halting only to hammer on the table or to stand with legs apart, swaying up and down as though to give weight to his words. Occasionally she felt the warmth of his foul breath on her face. She stood motionless, following his actions, and at the same time feeling some concern for his fine riding breeches: they fitted so tightly over his rear and his movements were very violent.

She insisted that she was no Communist. That couldn't harm anybody and was furthermore the only statement that she could give with the conviction of speaking the truth. He did not believe her, and changed his tactics, telling her that this one and that one had said this and that, so there was no need for her to take them into consideration. He told her that she could be transferred to the open section within the hour if she would just give the smallest amount of information about this or that. Grandma nodded to her energetically. Respect for the commandant prevented her from cutting into the conversation, but her whole bearing clearly entreated: "My child, now be sensible!"

Tora seethed. She retorted that she was perfectly satisfied with her present quarters, and the interpreter stammered out her reply. The ceasefire was over. The commandant had ceased his contortions and now stood over her threateningly. "Will you or will you not speak?" "I have nothing more to say." "Damned Communist pig! You'll be shot!" "It takes more than bullets to frighten a Norwegian." The interpreter gaped, while the frenzied ringmaster appeared to fight for air. "We'll wring the truth out of you, like this!" Choking, he ripped a newspaper to shreds. "We'll break every bone in your body, like this!" A ruler snapped in two. Tora felt that her body was a taut bow, stretched to breaking point. "Very well, go ahead." "Get out!" The air trembled with the sound. She had a fleeting glimpse of the astonished gaze of the office girl as she left.

She was exhausted beyond belief. She listened to Grandma's retreating footsteps and fell forward onto the table, eyes and voices, words and papers whirling crazily round in her head. Blue cigarette smoke undulated, drifting across leather-patched riding breeches being slapped with the two halves of a broken ruler. The interpreter's nervous hands broke a leg encased in a shining leather boot. A giant staring eye hovered over Grandma's head. Now to sleep, sleep, sleep....

"Food!" Grandma stood at the table, shaking her. Tora was not hungry; she wanted only to sleep and fell onto her bed.

Is Grandma still here, still shaking her, even though she has said that she wants no food, only to be allowed to sleep. What is she saying? Get up? Quickly? Quickly?

The old woman handed her her clothes. Harrying. Tormenting. What is it they want? Is it the ringmaster again? Coat and hat too? Out, now? She looked at Grandma imploringly. "Yes, quickly!"

Now it was coming. The avalanche. Tora prayed--a wordless, formless prayer. Grandma was pressing good advice upon her. Many had thanked her for that advice in the past, had saved their lives by following that advice. Just confess. It's the only way. There is no person alive that can stand up to the treatment of the Gestapo. It would be madness to allow herself to be an invalid for life just to cover up for others. She loves life, doesn't she? Life--it's so beautiful. She doesn't want to be shot, does she?

Grandma continued to talk in a normal everyday voice; she might have been accompanying a departing guest to the door.

Tora was calm; her fear had vanished. She walked on, and as she passed along the corridors she sensed a growing understanding of a mentality she had hitherto refused to believe could exist.

Two male prisoners were sitting in the car. They were silent. One of them was in handcuffs, which rattled slightly at every turn. The other twisted a handkerchief in his large, dependable-looking hands. She saw that they were both shivering in their thin summer clothing; but she did not think to cover them with her coat.

Five

Victoria Terrasse. An elderly guard was sitting in the outer office. He was wearing a uniform but had none of the Prussian mien. His lined face was thin and grey and she noticed his scraggy hands and protruding veins. His eyes were kind; his look was one of profound dejection.

The male prisoners were escorted by one of the Gestapo men from the car. The guard led Tora to a cell far into the basement. He handed her a cigarette and as he lit it she turned away from the sorrow in his eyes; she was so moved by the unexpected kindness that she dared not speak. He turned the key softly and left.

Tora's head began to swim from the cigarette. The cell was quite empty--no chair, no bunk. She sat on the floor and inhaled deeply, thinking of the guard.

Why doesn't he risk being shot rather than working for these hangmen? He had worn a wedding ring. Was it right to let consideration for others count for more than truth and justice? No, she could not believe that; but it was probably different for those who think only of this life on earth.

Where was Harald? She would always remember his face and voice when he had said, "I must go." She tried not to think of it, fearful that he might be able to sense her thoughts and understand her pain. No--she must not think of Marit either.

52

She lived not very far from here. The cigarette burned her fingers. It was cold--best to move about.

Somebody was coming. A cell further along was unlocked. She heard screams and shouts, then running, followed by a thud against a wall. Silence. She listened, breathless. Was it her turn now? No--they started up again, now with a whip. She heard the whine as it rent the air before cutting into flesh. The blows were followed by unimaginable sobbing broken by choked groans. Merficul God--make them stop! Let them come here! Anything to stop these terrifying sounds.

Suddenly, all was still. Was he unconscious? He must not die--don't let him die! They were leaving. She strained to hear a sound from the prisoner. "He got too much that time, blast him," one of the devils remarked as they passed.

When the guard arrived to fetch her she was lost in her thoughts for the mother of this young boy. Her mind was fixed on this unknown woman. In her imagination she stroked her hair, implored her still to believe in spite of everything. The boy had not died in vain: his was the highest human sacrifice, that he had fought to the end for freedom and justice She must always remember that. She felt the tears of the mother running down her own cheeks.

The guard was standing in the doorway. She followed him serenely.

It was the same office as on her first visit, and the same five men were assembled. The sight of the little grey fellow gave her a curious strength. He seemed agitated. She took the first move and spoke up clearly. "Good evening!" They all looked at her.

The grey one started up: "In a more cooperative mood, I hope. Will you now explain to us what you know?" He toyed with a long, black object which was lying on the table and which she assumed to be a rubber baton. "How many times do I have to repeat that I have nothing more to say?" She looked directly at him. He moved to stand directly in front of her. There was a curious yellowish gleam in his eyes. "Nah, speak up!" The blow was so unexpected that she reeled, struggling to maintain her balance. Her hat came to rest by the door and her hair fell to her shoulders in a shower of hairpins. She was determined not to scream, certain that was what was expected of her by this monster; she was not going to give him that pleasure.

"Nah, not yet?" A volley of blows rained on her--about her ears, on her neck, the back of her head. She staggered; then planted her feet astride, bracing herself to stay upright. She looked at him. The man must be mad: his expression grows more and more savage as the assault continues. If only he would aim at her body. The pain was intense--she was dizzy. Her assailant paused and she brushed her hair from her face. "Nah, have you had enough?" She attempted to straighten up and looked at him. There was no defiance in her gaze, only a deadly earnestness. "You can carry on until you've beaten the life out of me, I still...." The last words drowned in a hail of fresh blows.

He was sweating from his exertions; droplets ran down his brow; his face glistened. A strange mist seemed to float before her eyes.

"She had never fainted. She was determined not to faint, determined not to scream. Her head felt so strange--there was a strange buzzing. The mist cleared; but there was no letup in the beating. She could hear his short gasps for breath--all else was strangely silent--only his breathing, and the blows, and the buzzing inside her head, and--"Nah, speak now!" There was a demented look in his eyes. It was as though with each blow he was willing her to scream: scream, damn you--scream, damn you --scream--scream--!

"If you don't wipe that bloody expression off your face I'll kill you," he suddenly shouted, and struck her with such force that she lurched to one side. She had a sudden glimpse of the man dressed in brown--eating.

Herring, mouthwatering herring--and beer. She felt herself swaying--falling against the wall, her head ringing.

The blows had ceased. Her hair stuck to her forehead. The men sat at the table, in deep discussion.

The one in blue looked dejected and ill at ease.

The one with the hard but not entirely unfriendly face appeared to be engrossed in a map on the wall.

The pale young collaborator was highly agitated. He must have been drinking--or afflicted with the same madness as his grey companion.

They debated whether to continue or carry on. "No, to hell with it--it's four o'clock," the grey one said, advancing to the door. He was quiet now, his fury spent, and he looked tired.

The one dressed in brown was difficult to fathom. He crawled around on the floor, picking up her hairpins. He brushed her hat off carefully before giving it to her. He offered her his arm, wanting to help her out, but she looked at him and said that she needed no help. His face gave away nothing.

She could just manage to walk by keeping close to the wall. Her head throbbed with every step. The pain was not unbearable, but spots danced before her eyes and there was a continual buzzing in her head.

She experienced a sense of elation at having said nothing; it filled her more and more and she no longer felt any pain--just incomprehensible gladness. As she sat in the car she imagined what her feelings would have been if she had not managed to hold out. Good God, what pain that would have been! Think if she had been afraid. Think if she had let something slip at the first interrogation. Their lying was so clever that anyone could have fallen for it; but she had lied back and said that she was amazed that the police, the so-called guardians of the law, could play so false. This seemed to cause a certain amount of unease, so that she gained a small advantage; but it wasn't always possible to think quickly enough. She knew that this was not the end, but was incapable of thinking about it any more. "They'll just have to beat me to death."

She waited in an office with an Austrian guard. "She can sit," the man in brown said. In any event, she would not have been able to stand. She recalled that she had once drunk too much champagne and realized that the sensation she was experiencing now was exactly the same; her body seemed to float, she wanted to laugh. The dark gaze of the guard was one of endless sorrow, but she felt no sympathy for him. "It'll do you good," she thought. "You can leave. You know what's going on here--night after night. You've treated me as nothing more than a parcel this evening, a mere parcel--with a Receipt of Delivery note attached for signature. Where are the other two? Why don't you tell what you have seen? Why are you so afraid for your own life? Your Norwegian parents--those who adopted you--didn't they give you life twenty years ago? Is this your way of thanking for that? Have you no conscience?" She wanted to hammer on the table and unleash a storm of reproach. She wanted to....

Funcke appeared. "Quickly!" The prisoner laughed, slithered along the wall and laughed hysterically. She liked Funcke. Funcke wasn't slimy. She wouldn't mind being helped by Funcke; but Funcke offered no help; she stood stiffly to attention, irritated and repeating, "Quickly, quickly!" Tora was drunk. "Champagne," she said, explaining in German and Norwegian that she needed the support of the wall. "They gave me champagne," she laughed, and tried to point at the head she could not feel. She had given away nothing. "They didn't manage," she thought, and tried to disperse the mist that seemed to float before her eyes with her hands.

Why was Funcke silent? Why didn't she help her? Why was she walking so slowly? Tora didn't want to go any farther; it was so dark down there.

Funcke helped her into bed. When had she undressed? She was no longer drunk. Funcke pulled the door to and gave her a cigarette, spoke to her; but it was difficult to hear.

Tora had known all along that she was kind, deep down inside her. Something had made her as she was--something had changed her. Tora asked if she was married. No. Is she? No, Tora was not married. "But you have a boyfriend?" "Yes, many." "Somebody special, I mean." "Yes." "Is he here?" "No--he's at sea," she lied. It was none of Funcke's business where Harald was. "I thought perhaps it was for his sake that you wouldn't tell anything." Take care, a voice whispered. "You can't tell anything if you don't know anything," she replied. That was not lying; she disliked lying--nor did she like this kind of cross-examination. In an attempt to change the subject she asked Funcke what she thought about Gestapo methods. And yet she was so tired, so tired; she wanted to be left alone.

She heard nothing of what Funcke thought; the woman looked at her silently, folded the blanket closely around her and left.

She was unable to sleep and unable to think. It was painful to close her eyes and equally painful to keep them open.

Funcke came with two sleeping tablets; she pressed them into her hand and gave her some water. She peered through the spy hole twice and when Tora smiled at her she came in. She wrung out a towel in cold water and laid it over her forehead. The pain was instantly alleviated and questions rose to the surface in her mind once more: why couldn't Funcke always be like this? Why do they take on this work? They must have seen so much--why don't they rise up in revolt?

Funcke appeared once more. "You should be sleeping by now," she said, "after those strong tablets." "It's impossible to sleep--I keep thinking...." "What are you thinking about, about those who knocked you about?" "No--about you." "Me?" "Yes--how you can bear to be in this place without rebelling against it all?" Funcke left without replying and did not reappear that evening; but Tora lay awake, looking at the hole in the cell door when the flap was cautiously drawn aside.

It was day and Funcke brought in the usual breakfast of bread; but Tora was nauseated by the thought of food and unable to eat.

The warder said that she need not get up; but it was impossible to sleep: the noises of the prison were so loud, the pain in her head grew more and more intense and the pillow was so hard.

Dinner was brought to her. She ate a little and threw up. Why can't they stop the noise! She was so tired. Funcke was behaving so strangely: she was angry, but still she came to look at her, saying nothing. She isn't really angry, inside; she is sorry. After supper she came once more with sleeping tablets. "Go to sleep quickly now. Goodnight." "Quickly, quickly!"

She was sick of that word. "Nah--speak up, now! Speak up!" "I've nothing to say." Grandma shook her harder. "I've nothing to say."

Six

It was Grandma--only Grandma. "Interrogation,"she said. "I'll never tell them anything. Never. They'll never get anything out of me." Tora had forgotten her head--until she began to walk. The pain was overwhelming. She clenched her teeth and started to walk, and walk--one careful step at a time.

She was in Dentzer's office. He flew into a rage as soon as he saw her, bellowing; but the words became one continuous roar and she understood nothing. The deafening voice was splitting her head in two. She clapped her hands over her ears and shouted with all the strength she could muster, "Don't shout like that! I can't understand a word!" There was a momentary silence. He looked utterly foolish and, gaping from her to Grandma, asked, "Is she completely mad?"

Tora could not understand his questions--would not understand them. She held her hands over her ears as he raged, and gave no answer. "We'll break you in the end." Grandma left. Dentzer gave Tora the order to march out. She straightened her back and stepped out. His heavy footsteps throbbed in her head and yet at the same time they were stimulating: she would not let him see how exhausted she was; she would show him just how much a Norwegian was able to endure.

She could not have had many minutes' sleep; the male prisoners were still up. She smiled at all those they met, but they appeared not to notice. They drew themselves up and stood to attention until they had been passed.

The man dressed in brown was standing outside a cell in the basement. He spoke to Dentzer, then turned to her and told her that she was to be confronted with Sørholt. She did not fully understand why, and tried to overhear their conversation. Dentzer wanted the cell unlocked, but the one in brown said, "I don't think it's a good idea that she sees him today--his bandages are pretty bloody." Was this true--or mere playacting to soften her up, get the better of her? She was ordered to stand on the far side of the passage with her face to the wall. A man was led out and she was led in. It was a single cell. An ordinary blue handkerchief had been spread on the table as a cloth and she was touched by its everyday appearance; they might have let her keep her own.

Sørholt was to look at her through the spy hole. She stood with her hands behind her back, put on a brave face and smiled as encouragingly as she could--if it really was him. That was all.

The man dressed in brown accompanied her--not up, as she had expected, but out. He signed off for her, as from that night, for the benefit of the Austrian with the inscrutable eyes. One of the boys from yesterday was sitting in the car. He was still handcuffed, but it was his hair that made the greatest impression on her: never had she seen anything so lifeless; it was as though it were covered by a grey veil. She was freezing. They might at least have let her keep her coat on. What would the night bring?

The man in brown got out and spoke to the driver who was cranking up the motor. She gave her fellow passenger's hand a swift squeeze and asked him in a whisper how things were going. "This is the fourth time I've been had up for inter-rogation." "What do they do?" "They use a leather strap, knot-ted." "Is it terribly painful?" "I'm almost used to it by now." The voice was toneless, as grey as his hair. The Gestapo came back to the car and they drove off.

The fourth time. How much can a person stand? Was it possible to get used even to torture too? A knotted leather strap? She would rather have that than things done to her head; it felt as though something was broken inside--that was what it felt like. Poor devil--the fourth time. No wonder his hair was lifeless.

The stop at The Terrace seemed very short this time. She prayed silently, continually, that they would both manage to hold out.

The same old guard was there that night also. Tora remem-bered his kindness and smiled at him gratefully. She would have liked to say something to him on the way down to the basement; but it was so painful to walk that she could not speak. "You're very pale--are you in pain?" he asked, pointing at her head. "Yes--great pain."

Shortly after, he appeared with another guard and they stood in the doorway talking. They seemed to be discussing the way she had been treated. She had difficulty in keeping her eyes from the cigarette dangling in the guard's mouth. No-ticing, he took out a cigarette case; but it was empty. He asked her if she would like the one he was smoking--his last. As he left the cell he dropped a matchbox onto the floor and let it lie there. It contained eight matches. She placed two matches and a small piece of sandpaper to one side for whoever might come after her, and stuffed the rest into her shoe.

It was bitterly cold. The cigarette warmed her a little and helped her to think calmly of what was to come. She gave herself some good advice, although it was not the same as the advice she had been offered by Grandma. Don't give them any information, whatever happens. Just stick it out. They must give up sooner or later. The fourth time, he had said. You're strong. You'll manage all right. And if you should die....

Tora tried once again to get her thoughts into some kind of order. That others should suffer, that was no better; no, it wasn't. She loved life; she did not want to die. Yet if she did not manage to hold out, then others would be taken. Once they had the thread, there was no going back. It was like a ball of yarn; they would unwind and unwind, through a labyrinth of mindless torture, over dead bodies, on and on. No--never!

The guard came; but he did not say, "Quick! Quick!" She clung to the wall of the passage for support. As she passed, she noticed in one place that the King's monogram had been scratched into the wall: "H7," the symbol of freedom. A glimpse of the King, photographed standing by a gnarled birch, flashed across her mind. His face had been filled with suffering. He had done the only right thing. Now she understood, although her first reaction to his escape from the country had been different. He must have been strong: it would have been easy to avoid criticism by becoming a martyr --but of far less value. "Alt for Norge." Would she ever see another birch tree? Why had she not lived more in accordance with that truth she knows is the only truth which can bring happiness to human life: "Do unto others as you would be done by."

There was a smell of something burning--hair--or nails. "Do unto others...." Lord God, help me not to hate!

The small grey fellow was completely on edge--much more than on the previous day. What had he done to the victim before her?

"Now, Frøken Halle, is your head better or does it need further treatment?" He gave her a malignant smile.

This day's interrogation was more thorough than on previous occasions. They each took their turn and were more ingenious than before; it was intensely tiring. All five kept a close watch on her face. They lied. Suddenly one would cut in: "You're lying--that wasn't what you said earlier!" or, "He had a cast in his left eye before!" She was not the least unnerved. "Then you must have remembered wrongly. He was wearing a grey suit; I distinctly remember the grey-green color of his cap--and how terrible it was together with the grey." She hoped that nobody was going around with that particular color combination! "And it was the right eye that had the cast. I'm quite certain. I have a weakness for cross-eyed people; there's something so touching about them. And he seemed to have a sense of humor. I like that too. That's why I noticed him particularly. That kind of thing is so rare nowadays--a sense of humor, I mean." She looked gravely at the one they called the boss. He turned towards the window. What was he looking at? The blackout blind was drawn.

The little grey one did not care for all this talk. Wretched girl! None of the boys involved knew this cross-eyed individual: she was just lying.

They carried on, reconstructing the entire account once more. "Incredible," the commandant said, finally. She gave him a look of weary resignation and asked, did he not think that life was altogether incredible nowadays?

The one in brown led her to the basement. "Frøken Halle, you are trying to convince us that you are stupid; but, God damn you, you are the craftiest one we have had!" He looked at her sharply, hoping to have hit the mark. She put on the look of agony, leaned against the wall, pale and suffering, pretending not to hear. It was not difficult; the pain in her head was agonizing.

She was immediately fetched up again. It was an endless struggle to mount the stairs. She was overcome by resignation and indifference, and a feeling that she would not be able to carry on much longer. She sensed a change in the atmosphere, knew that something was drawing near.

They started up anew. This time they let out details that she had no idea were in their possession. The situation was becoming dangerous and she knew that she must be silent; using her head as an excuse, she said that she could stand no more. "You're not getting out of here this night until you have told us everything you know," the one in grey hissed. She was wondering if a few tears would help when one of the men suddenly leapt behind her, threw a towel over her head and bound it tightly, leaving her nose and mouth uncovered.

There was a sound of metal rattling. They were on the floor in front of her. Her right leg was straightened out. What were they going to do? "Pull your dress up!" She stiffened, remaining motionless. Somebody was fumbling with her dress. She felt fingers--first fumbling at her leg, then fastening something just below the knee. Something hard. "Will you talk now?"

"You know I've nothing more to say." It was strange that her voice did not tremble, for inwardly she trembled.

A screw was turned. "Nah?" There was no response. Another turn of the screw, and another, and another. Harder and harder. "Nah? Nah? Nah?" She gripped the chair with both hands. There was a feeling as though her skin were splitting. It was painful. Very painful. They asked questions, questions about everything she could not reveal. "Nah!"

Another turn, then a pause. Just keep on asking.... The pain travelled in a fearful shudder down to her toes and up through her thigh, gradually seeping through her entire body. She was overcome by a strange sensation of being divided into two: it was as though her real self were suspended in space. She no longer felt any pain--only a pervasive numbness.

Judging from the voice, the grey individual was sitting on the writing table immediately in front of her. They started up again. Who was turning the screw? A voiced whispered close to her ear: "We shall continue to tighten the screw until every bone in your body is broken!" The pain was so intense that tears began to soak into the towel and perspiration to trickle down her back. "Damn and blast you!" The screw was suddenly kicked up, then down. Up--down--up--down. Her body was racked by a piercing, throbbing pain. "Nah?" Every nerve seemed to writhe and twist.

She folded her hands in her lap. "Dear Lord and Father, help me!" She knew full well that she would get the help she needed, but prayed aloud: it would do them good to hear her prayer, to know the source of her strength, to know that she was not alone. The silence was shattered by shrill, hysterical laughter: it was the young collaborator. "Ah no. Our Father can't help you as long as you won't talk," he laughed."

"It's not difficult to see that you don't believe in any God since you dare to do these terrible things." Her voice was shaking a little now. No one replied. Another turn of the screw. "How long will the leg hold?" "There it goes...." "Rot! A leg can take a lot." But there is a limit. No! No more.... Tears were streaming into the towel. Her mouth began to tremble. Her body was growing steadily colder. The turning of the screw ceased.

She would not have believed such happiness possible, not

as it was at this moment. She sat massaging her leg--up and down; she did not want it destroyed for the rest of her life. "Shall we take the other leg straight away?" The one in brown asked the commandant as he removed the towel.

"No." His voice was subdued. He stood with his back to the room, facing the blacked out window. She rubbed her leg. She was filled with gratitude and exultation.

They discussed what was to be done with her, if she should be taken to the surgery. "No, goddam it--nothing works on her!" she heard one voice say. What happiness to hear it!

She tried her weight on her leg, but it would not bear her. The one in brown was waiting. He wanted to carry her out to the waiting car. In his arms? Never! The leg was not broken. Of course she could walk on it. Nonsense! Pull yourself together.... She hopped along, close to the wall, dragging the other leg lifelessly behind her. The stairs were almost impossible to negotiate. The one in brown was getting impatient, tried to drive her. "Be quiet--you had plenty of time just now!" He stopped, taken aback by her tone. I'm learning from them already, she thought.

The old guard was standing at the door to the outer office and looked at her, horrified. His whole aspect was so dismal that she was tempted to give him a barely perceptible wink. "Get inside!" the one in brown snapped. The guard turned and disappeared.

They drove off. She was filled with jubilant happiness. She had managed it--this time too! The prisoner with the grey hair had got into the car after her. How had he managed? His face was unchanged. His hair too; not burnt at least. His hands? They were hidden. She remembered the matches. She massaged her leg, got hold of the matches and stuffed them into his pocket. "What are you up to?" The one in brown half turned towards them.

"Are you going to stop me from massaging my leg too?"
The male prisoner shivered. Was it the cold? He was so pale.
Nerves perhaps....

Perhaps this was how one became after four treatments.
She thought about what might lie ahead. She was no longer
afraid: she had come to the conclusion that when the pain had
reached its limit--when it could hurt no more--then what did
it matter how it was inflicted?

They picked up Funcke a short way from the guardhouse.
So she lived outside--in which case maybe she really did not
hear what went on at night. She had to sit on the lap of the man
dressed in brown. She sat upright, unapproachable. He attempted to put his arm around her waist, with no success. Tora
wondered if he was just as keen on all women. He alighted
first, together with the male prisoner. "You'll have to take care
of the other one," he said to Funcke.

She backed away as she saw Tora totter helplessly from the
car. "So, tonight too," was her only comment. Her voice was
cold as ice.

Tora was limping; but she did not feel her head, nor her
injured leg: she was full of happiness and an urge to embrace
the world. She would have embraced Funcke, but the woman
was stiff and unbending, and made no move to help her. Why
not? Was she afraid that any offer would be refused?

"When did they fetch you?" she asked. Tora stopped
briefly; there was no barking "Quick! Quick!" from Funcke
now.

"Shortly after you had gone." The warder looked at her
watch. Four sleepless nights.

"By whom?"

"The old woman."

In the cell she stood talking for a while. She asked what they had done.

"Nothing more?"

What can she mean? Doesn't she think that was enough? It was--far too much. Inhuman. Diabolical. Medieval. Funke did not contradict her: instead, she asked, "Do you hate them?"

"No, I believe in God. I do not want to hate. Only love can change human beings and the world for the better." Funcke turned and left.

The morning round began. Tora sat motionless all day. The reaction began to set in: she was engulfed in pain, every nerve vibrated. Her head felt like a festering carbuncle, splitting and roaring. Her leg throbbed--her whole body throbbed. With no strength to massage her leg, she sat, nauseous and spent. Her eyes felt stiff and as though filled with sand.

In the late afternoon she heard the sound of a whole pack clattering along the corridor: the stamp of boots, angry, berating voices, with Dentzer's roar rising above the others.

Suddenly the cell was full. There was no time for alarm; it had all happened with such overwhelming speed.

Dentzer played the leading role. Four Gestapo men and three female warders made up a neutral, supporting cast. She herself was the prompter, desperately hoping that she would not be called on to say anything. It seemed that the sight of her was enough. Dentzer was revelling in his role; but a dozen leading men could not get her to stand on that leg.

He towered over her like a mountain, waving a riding crop under her nose. "So, you remain sitting. Sitting--when the Grini commandant comes in! Do you imagine that a wretched cretin like yourself can stand up to the German Security Force--the German Security Force! We'll break you--break every bone in your body!" His glaring eyes rolled. The riding crop brushed her nose. She rubbed it with a finger and looked at him expectantly, waiting for the next line.

He fixed her with a glowering, bullish stare. Doesn't the woman realize how angry he is? Furious! Exasperated! He grasped the pillow and hurled it violently through the door. The supporting cast flapped nervously to one side. The blanket was flung out. The mattress he had to carry, his face scarlet. His jacket strained across his back. His well-nourished hindquarters bulged in the splendid riding breeches. He groaned and spluttered like a whale.

A growing desire to laugh welled up inside Tora. Uncontrolled anger always affected her in this way. She knew many violent-tempered individuals. She called such behavior a lack of self-control, but this was not much cared for. A violent temper had a better ring to it.

A circus like this could never frighten her. Now he was standing, legs astride, the commanding officer, surveying the battlefield with eagle eye. What next? The curtain cord. He jerked it with such violence that she expected the wall to fall about her ears. Only the curtain came away; the cord still hung in place. Revengeful, he cut through it with a small penknife; it seemed an incongruously innocent act in the world of this fortress. "There!" With two resounding steps he reached the door and disposed of her hat and coat. Out! Out! Tora thought she noticed a shadow of a smile on Freyer's face as she hastily got out of the way. With one last crushing look at the prisoner, he disappeared.

The tension slowly subsided and a blessed silence reigned. Tora thought of steady rainfall after thunder. Was it possible that he had really meant it--that he was serious?

In the silence, she felt pain. It didn't matter: they hadn't succeeded--so far.

Seven

The evening round was over. Aren't they coming soon with bedclothes? She was overwhelmingly tired and unable to sit up any longer. She took off her dress and lay upon the bare bed. A cold draft from the floor came through the uneven wooden slats.

Grandma was there. "Get undressed!" "Get undressed," not "Get dressed." Relieved, Tora folded her few garments neatly. Grandma gave her a blanket, took her clothes and left. Perhaps they were going to inspect them?

Tora waited for the remaining bedclothes--and waited. They had so much to do: it all takes time.

At last Grandma returned. She glanced round the cell and took the towel and washcloth. Tora asked for the bedclothes. "Later," she said, and left.

This was too much to bear: after four sleepless nights, was she going to be forced to sit up because they could not be bothered to throw in a mattress and a pillow?

She rolled herself in the blanket. It would do them good to find her sleeping on the bare boards--when they came with the rest. The blanket was torn, rough. She felt it chafing her naked body. It had an evil smell. Who had used it before? Waves of nausea rose inside her.

Why -- why don't they come with the bedclothes! Her

head hurt the most: the leg was ice-cold and lifeless. Her head felt like a vast, open wound, and as she turned pain flared from her head and ear. She lay on her stomach with her head in her hands. Her arms were soon numb and her head throbbed. The blanket did not cover her completely; she was cold where she was uncovered and tried to turn it, but it fell to the floor. She sat up and leaned against the wall. The edge of the bed cut into her back. She wanted a mattress--and a pillow. Most of all a pillow. She must sleep. She could not bear it any longer.

What would happen if she threw the chair at the door? Again and again, until they came? The others would wake up; they would not know what was happening; they would be alarmed, unable to sleep more; they would lie awake, thinking. No.... She sat throughout the night. Nobody came with clothes.

She did not look up when the cell door was opened in the morning. Her clothes had been replaced. There was bread too; coffee had been forgotten. Her entire body ached. She was stiff. She was cold. She started to massage her throbbing leg, with tears and perspiration running. How much easier it would have been to give up, play the martyr. So much easier. But no, she must think of the future, if she ever got through this. She kept at it until the pain became unbearable.

Throughout the rest of the day she sat. Every time they looked in she was sitting at the table, her head in her hands. She had the feeling that it would break apart.

She realized dimly that she had been given no dinner. Bread was brought but remained untouched. She felt only thirst and drank water.

The evening wore on slowly. Still there was no bedding. The 'Mountain of Meat' appeared. "Clothes!" she shouted, pointing. Why did they talk like that, never a whole sentence?

Off, on, out, in, quick, food, later, wait.

"I must have some bedclothes first."

"Yes, later. Get undressed!" She drew nearer the table, and Tora began slowly to take off her garments, all except her vest. "Everything!" She had no strength to protest, nor to speak at all. Tora gave the woman her last garment to get her to leave.

The light was not switched off. Perhaps this was an indication that she would be given some bedding after all. Tora wrapped the blanket around her and sat on the floor, her back against the radiator. It was still faintly warm; but there was a cold draft from the grating underneath. She dozed, waking as she collapsed onto the floor. She was stiff, cold. She lay on her back alongside the radiator. It was completely cold by this time, but the floor retained a slight warmth.

Funcke found her in the same position in the morning. "My child!" she said, but the prisoner did not reply. Her head felt so strange. She had been wakened twice during the night by a violent eruption inside her skull, followed by a coldness which seemed to flow down behind her brow. She was unable to speak. All sound was pain. All movement was pain. She was faint and unable to stand.

During the day she remained sitting. Her mind was blank. She had tried to think, but this exacerbated the pain. Therefore she did not think, but merely sat.

At night she lay on the floor, continually turning. She awoke instantly at the sound of heavy boots or a slamming door, the knifelike sounds seeming to pierce her head. She dozed fitfully, but the sounds were always there. Nobody came; but she knew that it could happen--at any time. There was nothing to do but wait.

One evening, bedding was brought in. She was amazed. What could it mean? Was the torment over? Was she to be allowed to sleep, to be warm? She smiled at the young girl who carried in a mattress; she looked like a child--perhaps eighteen.

"Quick!" Funcke was in the doorway. The young girl sent her a brief but intense look before leaving. Tora made up the bed, thinking of the girl. She must be a prisoner. She had not dared to look directly at her--just that cautious sidelong glance as she had left. And Funcke's tone of voice. Tora crept into the bed.

The mattress was full of the familiar large, hard lumps. Perspiring and with throbbing head, she attempted to arrange them as best she could to lessen the discomfort. It was sweet relief to be free of the scratching of the blanket against her bare skin, and to feel the coolness of the clean sheets. She turned her head cautiously on the hard pillow, and slept.

She slept peacefully through the night and awoke restored the following morning. Her body was stiff and the pain was still in her leg and head; but she was able to think and was filled with gladness.

Dinner was brought to her also. The young girl from the day before was clearly sympathetic. "Dry bread for four days?" She ladled the grey soup onto the plate until it ran over. Tora was filled with an urge to cry, to rest her sore head against the girl's arm, to show her her leg, now black and green from foot to thigh. What solace it would be to speak of her ordeal, to tell of the suffering and continual pain.

Instead, she smiled as best she could. The elephantine warder mumbled something and slammed the door. Was it the overflowing soup bowl that had irritated her, or the smile? Probably the latter.

In the evening her bedclothes were once more removed. The young girl did not look up. Tora understood. The huge warder seemed agitated as she stood fingering her bunch of keys, pretending not to see her.

She was unable to sleep that night and lay thinking over the methods used by her captors, vexed at her own unbelievable naiveness. They were fully aware of the psychological strain inflicted by this treatment. How was it humanly possible to devise such callous methods? First to bring food and bedding, with no explanation, after endless nights without sleep and days without food; to let the exhausted body delight in the sight of the bedclothes by day, when lying down was forbidden, only to remove them at the very moment the poor wretch has been waiting for. She resolved to be fooled no longer with their "wait" and "later." At last she understood that it was all a part of the penalty: no comb, no toothbrush, no outdoor exercise. She had asked four times to be allowed to cut her fingernails--and had been gullible enough to think that her request had merely been forgotten.

She turned over, pondering over how to best formulate her outcry--at her next meeting with the ringmaster--and hoping that it would take place while she still had strength.

The following morning she was visited by the man dressed in brown. He sat down and appeared friendly--so friendly that he opened a full cigarette case. He lit up, letting the case lie open on the table in front of her throughout the interview. Was this meant to be a temptation? She smiled faintly.

The stupidity of her behavior was aired once more. It benefits no one, merely makes things worse for herself, an attractive young woman with love and life before her.

She was overcome with an urge to slap his smooth, handsome face, time and time again, to put a stop to such talk.

He carried on: life can be so good, it's just a matter of adapting. Is she engaged? She gave no reply. He continued to speak in such a tone and manner that she was finally impelled to ask if the interview was supposed to be an interrogation. "Well, if you prefer the interrogation methods at The Terrace, that's up to you." He smiled.

Before leaving, he told her that Sørholt was one of the most obstinate fellows they had ever had to deal with; it was impossible to get anything out of him; they would have to destroy him in the end. It was crucial for them to track down the connection with the leaders, cost what it might. Her continued silence would only result in the two of them first being broken, then executed. "Think about that, Frøken Halle, you would be to blame for another person being put to death." This parting shot was delivered with utmost pathos.

She did think--for the rest of the day and through the night. She had not considered the matter from this angle before; Sørholt had a wife and child. So had the others. Could she perhaps help him by talking--a little? Surely he would understand that her silence is to safeguard the others? She could save herself and him from further torture--but they are cut off from the work outside; the importance of that outweighs all else--the work outside.

She must remain silent; there is no other solution. They could just be threatening her, playing their last card.

She fell to massaging her leg, thinking of Sørholt. Was this ordeal worse for him than for her? How do men stand up to the pressure? Physically they are stronger--but are they as resilient, does it take less time for them to break down?

She lay down cautiously on her back. She had never before known a floor to be so hard, or sounds so deafening; they seem to be repelled by a barrier deep in her inner ear, only to re-enter the body in shafts of pain.

She turned. Would she ever grow used to sleeping on the floor? Her back was so cold. A draft blew from the grating.

She hauled herself up and lay on the bed. Someone was walking in the corridor, looking through the hole in the door. Were they coming?

Whoever was outside went away. Why did they spy on her so often? Her heart beat unnaturally. She had never thought about her heart before, never noticed that it was there. It was colder on the bed.

She sat up unsteadily, limped to her place on the floor and stretched out, turning from time to time.

She heard a rumbling from the basement boiler room. It was soon morning; they wouldn't come now. She moved closer to the radiator, and slept.

In the morning Freyer appeared, together with another woman. An inspection. They looked into the cupboard, into the washbasin and at the prisoner. She stared back. She had made up her mind that if they asked her to get up she would refuse. No command was given and they departed. Freyer had been amicable and the other woman looked kind. She had smiling brown eyes and a liveliness about her instead of the familiar air of an automaton.

The other prisoners were being exercised. Tora yearned to get out. Snowflakes whirled softly in the air. Would she never again feel that fresh, cold air against her face--or go skiing? Harald!

She must think of something else. She focused her attention on the curious, random flurry of the snowflakes; they did not fall straight down, but seemed first to execute a lighthearted little dance in the upper air. She remembered a cabin, a sooty fireplace; a yellow pitcher filled with heather had stood on the mantelpiece. She remembered some tulips she had seen on the day of her arrest and saw once again their dark sheen in her mind's eye.

It was the dinner hour. Tora was given bread. She was heartily sick of it, even though they brought a different kind each day. Sourdough today. It had a different smell too. She chewed slowly, thinking of ham and eggs--thick slices of ham.... Her mind went back to such a meal, eaten in a small cottage deep in the pine forest. She saw the black pan and the thick, crisp slices, the fat streaking the delicious gravy with transparent rivulets.

Grandma came. She stood staring at the prisoner, who continued her chewing. "You seem to like it," she said, in an irritable tone.

"Yes." Tora chewed and swallowed, taking her time. "You see, I learned a lesson from my mother: she used to say that all food was good--and bread is food."

Poor Grandma--she couldn't know about the ham Tora was enjoying. She gaped at Tora uncomprehendingly, shook her head and left.

That evening she heard the dreaded order again: "Get dressed!" She tried to tell herself that she was past caring, past all fear; but her heart was hammering, hammering. She pulled on her garments with trembling hands, turning away so that Grandma would not see. She had already seen--she was smiling and thinking, tonight she will give in, she has held out for a long time, but now she can't take any more. I knew it. They all give in--in the end.

She led the prisoner gently to Dentzer's office. There was a feeling of something delayed--only as far as this office-- for the time being. Grandma remained standing beside the door. This could mean that she would be taken back to the cell--for the time being.

Dentzer started up with his well-known theme: Communism, her foolishness. He moved on to her responsibility for Sørholt's destruction. So it is decided. "Think of his wife and children, what you are inflicting on them. Think of what it will mean--no breadwinner for the family. Small, helpless children!" Yes, he knows his stuff.

Tora grew more and more enraged the longer he continued. She asked to be allowed to sit; she had some things she wanted to say to him.

"But of course, of course!" He jumped up with a show of chivalrous concern and settled her in an easy chair. He glanced triumphantly at the old woman. Wasn't that just what he had said--that he could handle her? He glowed, sat down expectantly. He could hardly refrain from rubbing his hands together.

Grandma edged closer, interested. The prisoner sat contemplating her long fingernails. "I've been thinking," she began. Dentzer leaned towards her, listening. No wonder her voice was trembling: after all, this was a serious moment for her. "There's so much I don't understand." He nodded encouragingly. Just as he had thought: she had become entangled in something with no idea of the consequences. She looked at him intently. He took notepad and pencil. "Why can't I have a comb and toothbrush? Why am I not allowed out for exercise? How do you dare to treat prisoners in this way? Look!" She held out her long fingernails. "Why can't I cut them?" The notepad fell from his hands. "What kind of medieval methods do you use here? Barbaric! You should be ashamed. Talk about culture! Losing the family breadwinner! Small, helpless children!" The barrage of words flared about him. Now he would explode.

There was no explosion. He closed his half-open mouth and clenched his teeth so that the knotted jaw muscles were conspicuous. He looked at Grandma and pointed to the door with outstretched arm. They left. Without a word.

Tora felt relief. The expectant face had seemed so comical since she had known what was coming. He would never succeed in breaking her.

There was a new warder on duty the following morning, the woman from the inspection, the one with the smiling eyes. Tora lay looking at her. She was an unusual type and spoke rapidly in an incomprehensible dialect. Nevertheless, she was sure that the woman was kind, and made up her mind to like her.

In the afternoon there was a new sound from the passage: somebody was walking back and forth singing--"Give me your heart Mari-i-a." It must be the new warder.

Tora loathed the song. It reminded her of the first day the Germans were in the country. The girls in the block where she was living sang interminably--"Give me your heart...."

The new warder collected her clothes in the evening, but did not notice that she had kept her stockings on. Grandma appeared shortly and ordered her to take them off. "But the leg is badly injured! It goes stiff as soon as I lie down--and I'm so cold!"

"Give it a rub," she was advised. Tora attempted to appeal to her better nature, but to no avail; she took the stockings and withdrew. Tora wondered if they were afraid that she would use them to hang herself, fools that they were. There were plenty of other ways of taking one's life if that was what one wanted. Smash the light bulb, for example; use a piece to cut over an artery. That is not what she wants. She turned over. Tomorrow she would ask for the last time to be allowed to cut her nails; they could just have forgotten after all. She massaged her leg. If they answered "wait" or "later" one more time, then she would give up. Let them grow. She couldn't stand any more. Nor the door being slammed without a reply. The day after tomorrow she would ask for a toothbrush and comb, for the last time. Soap too. She turned over. If they did not give it to her, then she would not ask again. Perhaps that was the wisest thing to do, carry on as though one needs nothing, is able to manage without--until one day the heart stops beating. Rubbish! The heart doesn't just stop like that. The unusually hard beating was nothing to worry about--probably just nerves.

She had seen some pictures of South Sea Islanders with nails as long as their fingers. She had thought them revolting. Someone was coming from the men's unit. She shrank into the blanket and stuck her fingers into her ears to shut out the sound of the steps halting outside the cell. What had the South Sea Islander looked like? He had a long, pointed face too; but it wasn't a he, it was a she. She had worn a skirt. Where are they now? Have they gone? Many native men from the South Sea Islands wear skirts. So do the Scots--splendid tartan skirts. She took her fingers from her ears and listened intently. All was silent in the corridor. She was cold and clammy and did not fall asleep until the rumbling started up in the boiler room.

It was Sunday. This she knew because of the late start of the morning rounds. Funcke came with bread. She greeted her: "Good morning! Nice to see you again--where have you been all this time?" The door clanged shut.

How strange Funcke had been--almost as though she suspected Tora of ridiculing her. How could she be so mistaken? Tora had missed her. She had in a way become a stable part of her existence--probably because of those nights when she had shown that she was not totally inhuman. Tora had often heard the warders talking and laughing with the other prisoners. Why were they so aloof with her? Surely they could understand that since she was alone, her need for a friendly word was much greater.

Somebody came along the corridor and stopped outside her cell. Her heart missed a beat. They stood talking. Tora could hear snatches of conversation: "That little Halle,"they said. Did this mean that she was going to be fetched again? The flap was cautiously drawn aside. Tora sat deep in thought, but suddenly looked directly at the hole, whereupon the flap immediately fell into place. The eye had been beautiful, large and grey. She wondered who it could be. Nobody came in.

Tora sat thinking about the curious silence which reigned for a while in the corridor after food had been handed out--a drowsy lull of repletion. Now the others were resting. She looked at the bare bed. Was there anything more forlorn on this earth than an old-fashioned, empty, wooden bed?

Suddenly, there was a commotion in the corridor-- strange voices shouting at once. "Sixty-seven--how's it going?" Tora limped to the door, interested and excited. Now they were shouting again. Why can't sixty-seven answer! "Hi--you at the top!" There was no reply. "You in solitary!" Her neighbor began to hammer on the wall. Perhaps it was she they meant. She began to tremble, tears stung her eyes. She leaned against the door, frantically clutching the jamb, and shouted: "Yes, I'm here!"

She had mustered all her strength, but her voice seemed to come from the depths of a steel drum. She tried to clear her throat--"I'm all right!"

"We feel so sorry for you--we're all thinking of you!"

She was totally overwhelmed by the knowledge that somebody was sorry for her, was thinking of her, somebody who knew.

Another voice called out, "When we knock three times on the wall, stand up on the window sill and stick your head out!"

There was a rattle of keys and a door was unlocked; then dead silence in the corridor.

She sat thinking that it would be impossible for her to stand on a chair. Her head swam at any attempt to limp. She looked at the window; the thought of standing on the sill was enough to make her break into a sweat. She was glad to be able to sit, using the table and wall for support.

She went to bed early that evening. The sudden discovery that somebody was thinking of her had drained her strength. She clutched the blanket around her and crept into a corner of the bed. Somewhere a door was opened. She heard music. Music--here! A song recital. She recognized the familiar voice of Erna Berger singing an exquisite lullaby. The music encompassed her and her silent tears began to flow.

Someone grasped the door handle. She hastily brushed away her tears. It was Grandma. "What are you crying for? Aren't you comfortable?" Her tone of voice was harder than the actual words. She said a brief, silent prayer before she drew a breath and tried to explain softly: the music...it was the music...she loves music. What was it that Erna Berger had sung? She had forgotten the title--it was so beautiful. "How did you know that was Erna Berger?" "How did I know? I heard it, of course--her voice is so well-known."

It was evident that Grandma was proud on behalf of Das grosse Vaterland. She looked at the prisoner--and at the bed. "Be sensible the next time, then you won't have to put up with any more of this." She went.

Why had it been for Grandma to remind her of the next time? She would not think about it--she would think about music. She turned over. She would think about clean sheets, a smooth mattress, a soft pillow. She tried to think of all the well-known operatic arias she could remember, all the performances she had seen, humming the melodies to herself. Harald. No--she dared not think of him. Music. She let her imagination wander back to orchestral concerts--was there anything more sublime! Her thoughts wandered at random--remembered conductors, remembered soloists. There is no pain in the sound of music. The sounds of the prison torment her. The sounds of the prison are hell on earth.

There is rapture in the sound of a great orchestra...like human love. Harald. No.... Yes, tonight she would think of Harald.

Funcke came with the bread, breaking into her reverie. Tora took her customary hold on the radiator and hauled herself up. She smiled at Funcke. "I'm managing very well, Frøken Funcke: in the evening I am so tired of sitting here that it's wonderful to lie down, and in the morning I'm so tired of lying down that it's wonderful to get up!" For once Funcke closed the door quietly; it was obvious that she thought Tora was quite mad. She looked through the hole in the door three times during the night--probably not used to the prisoner smiling at her each time.

Eight

Tora noticed that she was growing more tired every day. She was not troubled by the lack of food; it was far worse to be unable to sleep. And the waiting; and the dark avalanche always moving closer; and her head which would not get better. The leg was improving; she massaged and exercised it a little each day. She no longer asked for a comb, or a toothbrush, or soap, or to be allowed to cut her nails. She had finally realized that they had not forgotten, but that it was a part of her punishment. Was the surly behavior of the warders, with their constant snide taunts, also a deliberate part of the strategy? Grandma was constantly saying, "You should be crying, not smiling," or, "How can you be so cheerful when you know you may be fetched for questioning this evening?" Or "Black Maria," the enormous woman, with her endless, "You're stupid. Just you wait--you'll have to give in in the end --they all give in in the end." One night, when Tora had been given bedding, Grandma had come to fetch her clothes. Tora was already luxuriating in the rare comfort of the sheets. "You seem to be enjoying yourself!" "Yes--when I finally get to lie down, I like to really feel that I am lying down," she laughed, feeling the uneven mattress beneath her. "Well, enjoy it while you may. You'll most likely be fetched for questioning tonight." No one came to fetch her; but even so.... How can the old woman treat her in this way? Funcke at least does not stoop to these shabby tricks but goes about her work--upright, angry and cantankerous!

One evening Tora heard knocking on the wall--three knocks. She struggled unsteadily to reach up but her head swam and she was forced down. The knocking sounded again; then silence. They had given up, not understanding, perhaps even thinking that she wanted no contact. She lay for a long time, knowing that somebody was thinking of her, feeling a rush of tenderness for that fellow creature.

Eventually the day came when she was fetched by Grandma for more questioning. As they made their way along the corridor, she delivered a lengthy homily on the brutality of Communism, the merits of the Nazi regime, the wisdom and foresight of the Führer, and his mission as the savior of the world. Tora felt incapable of speaking to her.

There were only Gestapo personnel present at the interrogation. There was a repetition of the familiar threats and talk of execution. The prisoner was totally indifferent. Her only response was that she should first be allowed to brush her teeth and cut her fingernails--also that she would like to have the notorious last cigarette.

The interrogators gave up. They looked at each other. Tora was beyond trying to find out what they had in mind. She was tired and depressed, sick of being alone and pining for the open air. Let them shoot: nothing mattered any more.

The following day the other prisoners called to Tora again. She replied briefly that things were going fairly well and that she would knock on the wall when she was able to stand on the window sill. She also asked what she could do about her fingernails. "Bite them! Try the wall!" She hobbled back to the wall and the consolation of the chair. It was painful to speak and to attempt to understand what the others were saying. She was exhausted. She had tried biting her nails long since, feebly attempting to tear at them with her teeth, but soon had to give up. Now she tried dragging them down the rough surface of the wall; but the nails were too long and too soft and merely bent over.

Another afternoon, another cross-examination. This time she was fetched by the young singer--"Give me your heart, Maria...." In Dentzer's office she was exposed to a repeat performance of the previous interrogation; she was assailed with the customary invective, plus a few expletives hitherto unknown to her. She was allowed five minutes in which to think things over. She saw a chance to make her views known to the Commandant once more, but was soon cut short by a savage "Go to hell!" There was an immediate "Jawohl," from the singing warder who hustled her out. She sniggered and gave the prisoner a nudge and seemed in high spirits as she pranced along the corridor. Tora disliked these antics; she had not intended to play for the gallery, yet there was something in the behavior of the young girl which reminded her of a cheap music hall artist.

From time to time she was given dinner and bedding, only to be left without the following day; but she had gradually become accustomed to such treatment.

She could walk--with a limp but without too great pain, although a dull ache throbbed in her leg incessantly. In her joy and relief, she had greeted Funcke impulsively one day as she entered with her ration of bread: "Frøken Funcke, I can walk again!" "Of course you can walk!" was the curt reply. For a moment Tora regretted that she had borne her sufferings without complaint and wished that she had shown her the leg when it was at its worst. At the time, she had decided not to do so, believing that it would cause the woman distress and shame to see the treatment meted out to prisoners by her fellow countrymen.

In the course of time she felt sufficiently strong to try to establish contact with her neighbors. At least she had tried.... She managed to open the window and to stand on the sill. Her head swam but she steadied herself and clung fast. During the afternoon she heard the answering sound of the agreed three knocks. She hauled herself up and, with some discomfort, stretched her head through the iron window frame.

A curly head appeared at the nearest window. It was "Kari." The head immediately disappeared from view. The only thing she had managed to see apart from the mass of curls were two large, grey eyes. "Bibbi" was a warm voice and a glimpse of a pale, narrow face and fair hair. The third face belonged to a girl named "Ester."

Tora lowered herself painfully. The speed with which the faces had appeared and disappeared had made her quite giddy. Was this how they did it? She realized that she had not thought to introduce herself in her confusion--she had probably looked like an idiot! She sat thinking about them for the rest of the day.

She heard the sound of the knocking again in the evening; but the pain in her head was intense and climbing up to the window impossible. She lay on the floor, entreating them silently to understand. The sound of distant knocking reached her as she drifted on the verge of sleep.

Her state of mind began to cause her some alarm. From time to time, it appeared to be snowing in the cell. No--not snowing: now silvery, grey leaves were falling, falling.... First she had seen red rings, intertwining and spinning crazily. It hurt. The grey leaves were better--they were beautiful; she sat for long spells, gazing at the leaves.

There was something worse: it had become so difficult to understand when the warders spoke to her. Other sounds were as loud as ever; there was nothing wrong with her hearing. They did not believe her when she told them. Why should they? She could understand them well enough before.

The next time she heard the knocking on the wall she climbed up. A voice whispered in the dark: "Have you got a comb?" "No." "Wait!" She drew her head in and waited, looking out at the dark outline of the landscape. There was a faint glimmer from the snow. Now they were knocking. "Here--take it!" Something seemed to brush past her face. For this she was quite unprepared. What was it? Had it fallen down? Once more--"Now!" This time she managed to snatch at the object before it fell back. It was a stocking tied to a string. "Pull the string three times before you let go," she heard. She was shaking and weak at the knees from the effort of clutching at the stocking and emptying the contents onto the sill. She pulled three times at the string and released it, forgetting any word of thanks, then lowered herself thankfully to the floor. She was quaking: her neighbors could not know that she was checked on several times during the night. She examined her gifts: there was a folded note, part of a comb, and two pieces of bread--with butter in between.

Imagine--butter! Tora lay with her back to the door and

her treasures hidden under the blanket. She separated the slices of bread and scraped off a little of the butter with her teeth, feeling foolish, then pressed them together again and ate slowly, savoring each mouthful. Oh, how good the butter was! She lay the whole night with the bit of comb in her hand, waiting for the morning when she would be able to read her letter, oblivious to the hardness of the floor for a short while.

Could it be nerves--or the countless blows to her head. Tora found herself unable to comb her hair. Her scalp was encrusted with dried blood. She wept. Nevertheless, she treasured the comb, six pink teeth, and hid it in the most un-likely places. She took it out when she felt safe and sat looking at it, pressing it in the palm of her hand, and thinking of the three occupants of the adjacent cell.

The reading of the letter was an emotional experience. She had read it a hundred times. "Dear--dear! We think of you so much. They cannot carry on like this with you for more than a month." For more than a month. She could not remember how long she had been there. More than a month?

"Give the signal whenever you want to stand in the win-dow." Her throat was sore from the few minutes' exertion the previous day. They thought it was easy to jump up and down. They knew nothing of her head and leg, that she lay for many hours afterwards, trembling and unable to sleep.

She talked to them in her thoughts, explaining; but she was no longer able to tell them apart. Which one was Kari? Bibi--was she the one with the curly hair? It did not matter; she thought of them as a whole--something true, something good.

There was a commotion in the passage in the night, the din

of tramping boots and strident voices shouting orders, followed by the sound of a woman's desperate crying. When all was silent once more, Tora was left with a feeling of being utterly broken down, and unable to face the rest of the night in thought.

Tora heard the sound of high heels approaching. She hammered on the door, after which she stood waiting and trembling; it was the first time Tora had hammered on the door at night. She had to sleep....

The door was opened by Freyer. "Can I have something to make me sleep? I haven't slept for several nights." Her voice was cracked and barely audible. "Later," Freyer said, closing the door.

She dragged herself back to the window and lay down. Later.... Don't cry--once you start you won't be able to stop. Later.... Pain was clawing at her head, clawing downwards, sideways. Now it seemed to bore inwards, deeper and deeper.

Suddenly the door opened.

Freyer stood waiting. Tora crawled over to her, trying to cover herself with the blanket. She stretched out her hand but Freyer brushed it aside and pushed a tablet into her mouth, her fingertips barely touching the prisoner's mouth. The door was closed.

Tora lay motionless. Don't cry, don't cry.... The barely perceptible touch of soft skin against her lips had sent a tremor through her body.

A few evenings later, bedding was carried in. She gave Grandma an astonished look, as if to say: "I had them last night too!" The woman said nothing, but looked at her for a long time before leaving.

Tora lay down but could not rest; Grandma had looked at her so strangely. During the morning she had come to the cell with a group of men. They had stood in the passage while Grandma and another person in civilian clothing had seemed to block the doorway so as to prevent them from seeing the prisoner; but they towered over the old woman and at least four of them had looked in. One of the spectators had reminded her of the little grey fellow. She had dismissed the incident from her mind as nothing more than a routine visit. She was used to being stared at as part of the furniture, but always took care to stare back. This was not liked and often appeared to cause embarrassment.

Was she going to be shot? She had heard that prisoners were sometimes given better treatment during the twenty-four hours before execution. In her imagination she went through the procedure--step by step. Dear God, thank you for what has been. Help me through what is to come. Parents, brothers and sisters, family, friends. Harald. There were so many loved ones. She tried to reach out to them in thought, to make them understand that the work was something she had to do. She asked them to forgive all that was left undone. Implored them not to hate: hate was so futile, so destructive.

The night passed. She felt no desire to sleep. It was Funcke who came in the morning. "Frøken Funcke!" The warder turned quickly and went over to the bed. "Please--tell me what this means." She indicated the bedclothes. "Am I going to be shot?" "No, my child. It's over."

There was a sound of strange, gasping sobs. Funcke stroked, gently stroked the matted, greasy hair.

Tora was glad to be alive. The avalanche had receded--for the time being. The next one could come; she determined not to think of it; the important thing now was to regain some strength. She had slept for several nights in a row although she still awoke at the slightest sound from the passage. Her head was sore and continued to throb like a festering wound; nor had the ache in her leg subsided. But she had a toothbrush. She had a comb. She had soap. Dinner every day. She had even had a bath--in hot water, with a washcloth--two washcloths! And towels. Life was good.... She examined her short-clipped nails, whistling softly. She paced out her thirteen measured steps, rested, and carried on. She was happy--until the next cross-examination.

She faced Dentzer once more. There was nothing new, nothing in particular that he wanted; just to warn her not to think that the matter was at an end. She did not reply.

On the way back to her cell they met Freyer. She looked at Tora's cautious limping. A touch of sciatica? Her tone was concerned, sympathetic. "No, just so-called nighttime inter-rogation." The prisoner looked her straight in the eye, where-upon her glance wavered.

Nine

Tora liked the view from the cell. When she sat at the table she could see the tops of some spruces--thirteen in all. They were fairly widely spaced and their trunks tall and slender--so tall that they swayed in the slightest breeze. She thought of the sea when she looked at them and wondered what kind of tree was used for ships' masts. These must be perfect--they seemed so supple, swaying and swaying. She imagined that she could hear the faint soughing in the treetops; even as they swayed, they were serene.

The evening sky behind the trees was suffused with marvelous colors; often the palest of shades behind a faint vapor of frost, or an occasional icy glint of winter-rose and violet and blue.

But most beautiful of all was the play of moonlight through the treetops before the moon was fully risen. Once it had risen over the treetops, there was not the same magic in the full flood of light.

The night staff often saw her sitting at the table, supported by the chair. It happened that they asked her what she was doing. "Looking at the moon." They didn't believe her. How could they, for they knew nothing of the play of the moonbeams among the treetops.

She was able to see more as she walked her thirteen paces.

Standing at the window was forbidden; but nobody could forbid her to walk the cell. She limped slowly around--slowly, slowly as she approached and moved past the window.

A yellow villa was situated on a nearby slope, with a backdrop of blue hills. In front of the house the trunks of bare birches were outlined against the snow and an open meadow stretched down to the main road. The road emerged from a wood and unfolded, wide and comfortable, with even snow-drifts on either side, as far as a red porter's lodge, where it vanished. It reappeared below the house, where it seemed to make a brief request for permission to continue; but thereafter some of its friendly breadth had gone, its freedom lost. It made an irresolute curve before finally daring to continue up to the prison gates.

If she looked in the other direction she could see a small triangle--probably the courtyard--and part of a wooden fence. Forty-one unpainted boards. There were many strange knots in the boards. They formed curious figures and amusing pro-files. She was especially fond of a little boy she had discovered; she greeted him every morning and laughed at his upturned nose. His unalterable good humor and optimism made her think of how life had been before the war. Why was it that in those untroubled times when life had been good, people had been so cheerless, so surly in their daily dealings with each other? Why was it that people hoped to be treated with humanity and kindness by others and yet they themselves so rarely displayed these qualities as they elbowed their way blindly through everyday life? To right these wrongs for her own part as best she could, Tora prayed for her life to be spared.

It happened that she once saw a prisoner in the small courtyard. Grandma was there also. The prisoner was walking round and round--like herself, only more quickly. Her hands were thrust deep into the pockets of a heavy winter coat. The cold was bitter and the ground evidently slippery: the prisoner kept her eyes to the ground. Grandma was surveying the side of the building when she suddenly caught sight of Tora. Her stocky figure straightened, she held her hands to her sides and fixed her gaze on the window. Tora drifted slowly past the opening. Grandma looked angry. Tora smiled.

The next time she passed the window, Grandma was standing rigidly, still gazing upwards. A lighthearted urge to wave to her welled up in Tora--perhaps even blow a kiss! There was something comical about her--the small mouth, pursed, angry--a bulky, shapeless cap drawn well down over her head.

Third time round, and she shook her fist threateningly. Fourth round and a look of exasperation. The fifth round brought resignation: Grandma ambled back to the prisoner.

Tora smiled, with the clearest conscience in the world: so far she had not been given instructions as to where she should look as she goes about her daily wanderings. The prisoner had noticed her and looked up from time to time as she passed. She was young, which probably accounted for the apple blossom complexion in spite of winter and imprisonment. Tora yearned for color just as she yearned for music and tenderness; she gazed at the fair young face. A childlike merriment lurked behind the sweet smile, but she seemed frightened. Now they had gone; Tora had not seen them on her last five rounds.

Throughout the rest of the day, Tora daydreamed about the girl with the apple blossom complexion and speculated on why the unknown prisoner was exercised alone.

In the afternoon Grandma appeared. Tora--prepared for a confrontation--greeted her: "Why are you so angry today?

You're so much prettier when you smile!" Grandma did not deign to answer. Instead, she opened the cupboard, moved the cup so that the handle was pointing in the regulation direction, and left.

There was nobody in the yard the following day. She had looked forward to seeing them. Perhaps tomorrow.... She had seen the 'Mountain of Meat' and asked for a needle and thread to repair her stockings, but this had merely led to more of the "wait" or "later" strategy.

She had chosen a slogan for herself, taken from the German classics, and painted it on down-to-earth Norwegian toilet paper with pink toothpaste. It looked good on the shelf over the sink--"Mensch, grolle nicht!"--and it pleased her eye from every angle as she walked the rounds. As far as she could remember it meant "Don't complain!" Something in that line, she thought. Grandma had smiled the first time she saw it, pointing a warning finger and shaking her head. But her indulgence had protected the slogan from the sledgehammer of the 'Mountain of Meat'; also from Funcke's impatience to get rid of it before the next inspection. She could not understand why this small pleasure should be taken from her. The make-shift banner, with cheerful pink letters, broke the monotony of the grey wall. Moreover, she found it to be exemplary reading!

One day, Grandma brought her a parcel of clothes--her own garments, familiar, loved. She ran her hand affectionately over a red blouse, was overjoyed to see the black, candy-striped dress. She placed her slippers under the bed and laid out her night clothes. Thick ski trousers were hung up and ski boots examined. She hummed and whistled as she limped back and forth, trying to make the surroundings a little more homey. She changed and felt her body luxuriate in the little black dress.

Soon she was oblivious to the throbbing in her head, the hissing in her ears, and the nagging ache in her leg.

"Get dressed--put on everything!" Good God, was this another cross-examination at the Terrace? "Quickly now! Quicker!" Tora was perspiring; she couldn't find the button-holes, and when she did the buttons were too big. She was led out--a different way than earlier--into a large, roofless con-struction. The door was locked.

She stood there, trembling. Her reaction was so violent that she leaned against the door in order not to collapse. The cold, crisp air smelled unbelievably good. She noticed that her shaking hand, fumbling for something to hold onto was a translucent white. Her knees gave way; she slid down the door and remained sitting in the snow. The wind felt like a cooling compress about her burning head. She closed her eyes and breathed deeply. There was a smell of snow and a mysterious taste to the air; she had never before realized that there could be a taste to air.

She spent the rest of the day immersed in these impressions. Over and over again she experienced the taste and smell of the snow, felt the cooling touch of the wind. Later she realized that she had paid no attention to her surroundings before, and regretted that she had not taken the chance to do so.

Some time later she was brought up for more interro-gation, after having felt safe for a long time. On the way she speculated uneasily about what might have cropped up. Perhaps she was going to be confronted with somebody recently arrested? Perhaps more torture? Surely Sørholt hadn't given in--not now?

As though in answer to her unspoken questions, the man in brown suddenly announced that she was to be confronted with someone who had seen her outside Larsen's office. An abyss opened up before her; the landslide advanced towards her. "So that was where you fetched the money?" There was a slight questioning note in the voice. She looked at him. "When are you going to stop this playacting? First it was Counter 14, then Counter 18. And now I am supposed to have fetched it from somebody Olsen, or Larsen, or whatever you called him." Her voice was calm, tired and indifferent; if he only knew how she was trembling inwardly....

"They're on the scent. Dear God, don't let them find the thread! Please don't let me be confronted by Larsen. He might think that I've told them something, then that link would be broken." She grew calm through her prayers--sufficiently calm to face even Larsen without fear.

The man who was brought in was a complete stranger. The one in brown fixed his gaze on her, looking for the slightest change of expression. She thought it best that the unknown prisoner should know exactly where she stood in case he had indeed seen her outside Larsen's office. She looked at him closely before affirming that she had never seen him before, ignoring the signal of the man in brown to be quiet. He berated her on the way back for speaking before she was asked; she took pleasure in his tirade.

One Sunday morning, Tora was ordered by Freyer to pack all her belongings. She looked at the warder's expressionless face and wondered what was happening. Her every nerve quivered.

Freyer led her to a cell on the second floor, locked the door and left without a word.

Tora looked about her. Was she going to stay here? The walls were a repulsive dirty grey and the air close. It was dark and cheerless, and the sight of two bunk beds offered no comfort. From the window she could see only a courtyard, some unsightly barracks and a distant blue horizon.

All this she could have borne had it not been for the air of suffering that seemed to permeate the cell walls. She felt physically crushed by the atmosphere; it seeped into her body and flowed through her veins like a vicious, evil darkness. It filled her head, lungs, and nerves, leaving her devoid of her last vestige of strength.

They found her crying. Grandma asked her in a surprised voice, didn't she like it here? Freyer seemed perplexed. Tora made no attempt to stop crying; it did not matter to her any longer that they should see. She sobbed on incoherently about the ceiling, the walls, drenched in suffering.

Freyer and Grandma did not interrupt her but just looked at each other. In the end Grandma tried to comfort her: from here she could see the men prisoners.... Tora thought of Harald. He wasn't here. She sobbed that she wanted to go back to the slender spruces, the yellow house on the hillside, the little boy with the turned-up nose. Understanding nothing, they left.

The days dragged on. She cried no longer, but there was no spirit in her; she sat for the most part, motionless. The window was no longer a diversion, although when looking out one day she did think that it would be fun to have a pencil and paper. The prisoners often stood for hours at the same task-- chopping or sawing wood, digging a never ending ditch. They carry planks, resting at every tenth step, or hack randomly at the snow. Each operation was carried out so slowly that she could easily discern every movement; but she had no pencil.

The sight of the prisoners caused the image of Harald to stand out painfully in her mind, and the dreary barracks and the urge to draw made her long even more for the view from the other cell.

She was chilled to the bone when she was taken to the exercise compound. There was no longer any taste to the air-- or to the food. She felt no urge to speak, nor did she greet the warders with a smile. Their moods--angry, irritable, or con- cerned--were of no interest. She sat, dying a little with each passing day.

They said she was to be moved. She was not her usual self until she saw the trees once more--her trees--from a light, green-painted cell on the other side of the passage.

All was as before, except the boy with the upturned nose. But she had already found substitute companions: in one tree- top she saw Minnie Mouse, a rooster perched on another, and in the midst of a dense tangle of small branches sat a troll--a comforting Norwegian troll. She went to rest, grateful and happy.

Her head throbbed and she was unable to sleep. She lay watching a bright star. It was much larger than the others and shone with a steady, yellow light. At first it seemed to peer questioningly through the upper corner of the left-hand pane but later moved slowly and almost imperceptibly diagonally across the window. Amid the trembling darts of light given off by the other stars, it burned with a calm radiance. She finally slept, free from the weight of the tears and suffering of others. And it was good to awaken in that place.

Morning, noon, and evening rounds; they made a wel- come change from the familiar six footsteps.

A herring was put before her for dinner--an immense salt herring, dripping brine, complete from head to tail. Small pools of brine formed on the plate, scales floating. She fingered her spoon. Was it possible to clean a herring with nothing but a spoon?

She walked a few paces, glaring resentfully at the herring. Yet she was enticed and felt her mouth watering at the thought of its oily flesh. She straightened her shoulders and launched into a teeth-gritting attack, thinking angrily of all those outside who had no idea of the enormity of the task of cleaning a herring with a spoon. She scraped, trembling and sweating, feeling as though she was soaked in brine, stuck about with fish scales, the scales of this herring that preferred to swim on the table. She grasped it so firmly that her hand grew numb. All her grappling produced no more than a few unappealing grey tatters of fish; but these she struggled to digest for the rest of the day. Her brow grew damp in a wave of perspiration which gradually spread over her whole body. All for a few herring scraps. But it was a good feeling.

The intolerable thirst was good also. She drew it out, held the sensation close as it rose to a climax, before allowing it a little water. It was a strangely gratifying feeling to truly want something once more.

She walked round after round, reflecting, glad of her ability to live in the present, and on all she had to be grateful for, even in this cell.

She had not looked at her existence in this way in the past, before she had discovered life's meaning. Then she had lived in a world of waiting, living out only half her life. Nothing had come up to her expectations--least of all herself. She thought of that indescribable time of transition, when everything between heaven and earth had seemed to rise up to stand in her way. The peace that had followed was indeed "the peace that passeth all understanding."

Now she lived with that constant peace--even in suffering. All feeling was intensified. She wished for no change, even though her sufferings were intensified; love, work, friendship --all intensified in goodness and value.

Her mind turned to Harald. She imagined giving him a lighthearted kiss on the tip of his nose, saw the familiar look of the little boy who didn't like to be kissed just there. She was glad that she was able to love. Harald....

The sound of banging on the wall broke into her thoughts. Perhaps it was a prisoner wanting to tell that she too was there, and to say goodnight. She attempted to bang on her own wall but her knuckles hurt. She got hold of the spoon and struck the wall with it a couple of times. The banging from the neighboring cell continued. It comforted her to know that there was a fellow-being in the neighboring cell. Nevertheless, each signal was like a sledgehammer blow to her aching head, and she prayed that the noise would soon stop. She lay down and pulled the blanket over her ears, wondering who her neighbor could be.

The following evening she heard knocking on both walls. Tora pressed a towel to her ears and walked slowly round the cell. She wanted to scream, but it would have been to no avail; she had given a couple of answering signals to them both, but the insistent knocking continued. Are they deranged from being incarcerated for so long? She could not understand the reason for all the commotion, and felt that her head was being torn apart. She stood raging in the middle of the cell, wanting to claw down the wall, and wavered on the edge of hysteria when the banging stopped. She lay awake for hours with the noise throbbing in her head. She dreaded the evening of the following day.

It lasted for a few days; then they stopped. Tora was relieved. Her head was painful in any case. A tooth was aching too. It would pass. She tried to detach herself from the pain and walked about whistling until it became too intense. Then she sat down and looked at Minnie Mouse, at the comical, forward-bent ears and the little sniffing nose. The rooster swayed stiffly on his treetop perch. If he could only crow--he always looked as though he was just about to! As always, her gaze rested longest on the troll; his indistinct outline gave free play to her imagination.

Sometimes she would wander in the Hall of the Mountain King, or in the enchanted forest with the storyteller; they built a fire together in the soft summer night, and he told his tales.

Nothing would break her, nothing would blunt her. She had given little thought to her nationality before the war. She had now come to look on it as a duty to show strength and endurance to these machine-men, to show them that life holds more than the power in which they trust. They could torment the last vestige of physical strength from her; but her inner strength would never be destroyed. She would show them-- and even if they were too stunted to understand, she would continue on her chosen path. This she must do, to be true to herself.

One day Tora met a young prisoner in the washroom. "Don't you want to signal to me?" she whispered before the warder came to fetch her.

It was the prisoner who had been exercised alone: the girl with the apple blossom cheeks. She had thought there was something familiar about her. She felt less alone, knowing that "Apple Blossom" was in the neighboring cell; and in her mind, the puzzle of the knocking routine gradually began to fall into place.

She determined to learn the system of the knocking, regardless of her throbbing head. But how? She pondered over the problem throughout the day. It was of vital importance. Apple Blossom knocked and knocked. If the girl could only understand that she longed to reply but could not! She was despondent and at the same time full of good will for her young neighbor. Surely she could feel it reaching out to her through the walls!

In the basement bathhouse on Saturday, one of the young girls who patrolled the corridors was handing out soap. Tora saw her chance to give the girl a hasty message, to explain to the prisoner in the neighboring cell that she did not know the knocking signals. The girl nodded. She thanked God that she had managed it and whistled, relieved. The Saturday showering would have been a blissful high point of the week but for the constant hounding by the warders. They peered around doors, continually asking, "Not ready yet?" or barking the familiar and despised command, "Quick, quick!" Tora did not hurry. Even if she had wanted to, it was no longer possible: the trembling of her hands made it difficult for her to dress, and the mad chase of the bathing session exhausted her, so that her legs would hardly carry her up the stairs to her cell. She spent the remainder of the day recovering.

A few days later a scrap of paper was pushed through the spy hole: it was the key to the system of knocks. It seemed simple enough and Tora was eager to learn, but disappointment soon set in: after the first four or five knocks she lost count. Apple Blossom knocked and knocked. Tora mobilized all her powers of concentration and strength to grapple with the system, but to no avail. Apple Blossom kept up her efforts evening after evening. Tora made a few attempts to respond, but always with the same negative result. Her head swam with the effort and she was unable to sleep until the morning hours.

She made her next move on the following Saturday, asking the corridor patrol for a pencil. No--she was told--too dangerous; but she was given a stump later in the week. The situation had become almost as exhausting as a cross-examination. She had never before been anxious when the warders looked through the spy hole or inspected the cell. In this new and hazardous situation she found herself quaking whenever they came, and the existence of the pencil-stump made it difficult for her to feign innocence. The fear of being moved once more haunted her and she stiffened at the memory of the cell across the passage. Here, close to Apple Blossom, she was content.

Tora knew that being detained in this place must be a living nightmare for her young neighbor; she saw her eyes, heard her voice, and longed to comfort her, to enfold her in an embrace and say, "My child...." She must be feeling a desperate need to communicate with someone. Tora strived as never before, trying to keep up with the knocking and to take notes as best she could. Her head was splitting, perspiration ran, her body was tense with listening for the slighest sound from the corridor. The knocking echoed in her head through the night--rat-tat-tat-tat, rat-tat-tat-tat--the kaleidoscopic alphabet swirled in her brain. "I can't--not tomorrow." "No?" The disappointed eyes of her young neighbor appeared before her. "No! Do you hear me? I can't carry on any longer."

"Don't you want to keep in touch then?" "No. The whole thing is driving me mad!" She could see Apple Blossom, sitting inert, dejected. "Yes, yes, I do want to." Rat-tat-tat-tat, rat-tat-tat-tat. The carousel whirled on.

Ten

The days had begun to take on a regular pattern. Washing, dressing, the morning round, followed by breakfast of dry bread and ersatz coffee. Tora found that if she chewed slowly and dreamed of butter and pork, it tasted quite good. She seldom thought of any other kind of food but delicious, mouth-watering pork. Lately she had been seeing pigs everywhere--fine, fat pigs--on the concrete walls, in the clouds, on the grey cell floor. After breakfast followed the work of the day--bed making, floor washing. She then started on her customary walking. She sang hymns until she could no longer bear the sound of her rusty voice; then she whistled. Or she would say a short, silent prayer, dwelling on the same circle of loved ones each day. First Marit--who she knew had the most dangerous assignments, working night and day with no thought for herself. She must not be captured. Let her be spared to carry on with her work! She spent the longest time of all thinking of Marit. After all the others came Harald, held apart, kept for herself. She felt that she could permit herself to do this, since she never placed him first. Finally she prayed for all those she had met in prison. The little grey fellow, the man in brown: open their eyes! Make them understand!

Often after this ritual, her thoughts would stray to a student she had known. It was during the early days of the occupation, when the army of Germans was marching through the land. As they had stood, watching a hundred and forty marching soldiers, she had longed to get her hands on some sticks of dynamite. "And you call that Christianity! You call that love," the student had responded, indignantly. He was an ardent humanist. At the time she had answered "yes," although unable to give any rational explanation of her feelings. She knew now that that same young man was one of Norway's keenest resistance fighters.

When the weather was fine, the prisoners were taken out for exercise in the morning. This she enjoyed, even though the compound was little more than a cage, with thick walls and an iron door on one side, netting on the other, and a view of a high wooden fence. Occasionally she was sad, hearing the prisoners in the neighboring cage laughing and talking together; but then, remembering the time when she was never let outside, she would raise her eyes to the sky and her spirits would rise.

It was raining. An officer was putting some prisoners through a punishment drill. "At the double! At the double!" Flushed, panting, they shuffled by. The window stood slightly open and she could hear distinctly their gasping for air.

"Down!" They threw themselves down in the slush. They were ordered to snake forward on their stomachs. An officer placed a glossy boot tip on the neck of one not keeping sufficiently close to the ground. He increased the pressure. Tora was overcome by a wild desire to smash the window pane and scream, "Stop it!"

"Dear God, help us to turn away from hate." A crimson stain appeared on the snow under the prisoner's head.

She would no longer pray for the grey-clad interrogator, nor for the one dressed in brown.

On the following day she hesitated before saying her final prayer. "Go on.... No, I cannot. They are devils." "Pray even so. There is, or has been, some good, some time, even in those devils. That good can be rekindled--through prayer." But she was unable to continue.

She thought of the prisoners of the day before and wept for them. At last, her inner struggle over, she prayed--for the man in grey and for the man in brown--and for the wearer of the polished boots.

A peephole had been scraped in the blue paint covering the window pane and through this she had once seen prisoners from the open section being exercised. She had yearned to join them; there were so many amusing types. One had long, thick grey braids swinging loose; another had them wound about her head in a style that suited her well. There was a dark brown, bobbed head. So shiny! Her eye followed the brown bob until it disappeared from sight. A blonde in grey clothing was limping. Had they used the screws on her too? In the middle of the compound one prisoner was walking alone. There was an air of sadness about her. Tora wished that she could be with the prisoner, smooth away the traces of pain around her mouth, kiss the sad eyes, make her smile. Suddenly Funcke appeared in the doorway, barking "Quick! Quick! Quick!"

The midday meal consisted more often than not of storm soup. A couple of times a week they were served boiled fish, sometimes with a greenish hue and repulsive odor; but the skin and fat were appetizing.

The afternoons dragged. Tora had no duties. She only walked. Sometimes she peeped down at the male prisoners. There was one who passed by many times a day and seemed to nod up at her; but once she had discovered that his greeting was not for her, he was no longer of any interest.

She was often unwell. She vomited and had stomach pains. When she asked to see a doctor, the answer was always the same: "Yes--later!" There were doctors at the prison; she had seen them among the prisoners, with Red Cross bands on their arms. There was one she had grown almost fond of for the human goodness that seemed to radiate from him.

At times, wracked by the agonizing pain from her head and tooth and stomach, she longed for death; but always somehow managed to pull herself together. There were no sedatives to be had. "Later," she was told--always "later."

Every evening she tried to tap out signals to Apple Blossom. The process was as painful as ever, but she persevered. She gradually became more adept at the system of knocking and grew to understand an increasing number of words. She had learned a lot about her companion in the course of two weeks. Her name was Matti and she had been in solitary confinement for eight months. Tora had not yet been alone for three months and yet the time seemed an eternity. Eight months! Poor little thing. Tora thought about her all day long. Unable to forget, she relived all she had been told. They had taken Matti at night to the house by the roadside. She had expected to be set free. Freyer had stood waiting in an outer room. Matti, twenty years old, used to only goodness and love, had stepped into the room, trembling slightly. She was seized by two men and clubbed all over her body. She had been dragged across the floor by her hair, told that she would never see her mother again, then thrown into a basement cell. For the first week she could only crouch on her elbows and knees. She was alone for many weeks--alone with the fear that they would come back. Tora grew to love the girl for all the pain she had endured.

The toothache grew worse and worse. Tora was desperate. Matti said that she must ask again and again to see a dentist. It was the only way to get anything done in that place; but Tora had given up. Matti could not understand what it meant to have the door slammed, always to hear the same words: "no," or "tomorrow," or "later" in reply to her appeals, and then to wait but never receive any help. Matti was so young, with all the freshness of youth, and no idea of what it cost her to ask. Foolish Tora, not to ask.

One day, prostrate with pain, she lay slumped across the table with a towel wound about her head. Freyer appeared and asked if she was ill. Tora had not slept for several nights. Seething with rage, Tora asked her, "What do you mean by such an idiotic question?"

The following day she was taken by Funcke to the dentist. Funcke stood by the chair. The dentist thought that the tooth was infected and, to be certain, took an x-ray.

Two days later Freyer came to the cell, together with Dentzer. She announced that the x-ray had shown an infection. Dentzer continued, asking if she was now willing to talk. Tora's answer was as before: she had nothing to say.

"In that case, in addition to your punishment, you will not be allowed any medical or dental treatment. Do you understand?"

Tora turned away and walked slowly to the window. "Keep calm. Love thine enemy." Deliberately, she completed her circuit. She felt that the smile she gave him was one-sided.

Freyer looked away.

Tora was locked in an inner conflict, often delirious with pain. She became possessed by an uncontrollable urge to simulate madness. They could not have had a madman in the cells for years, so it should not be difficult. She wanted to be violent, to keep up a constant, resounding din, so that in the end they would have to send her away. How good it would be to hurl the stool at Dentzer's head the next time he appeared in the doorway!

Afterwards they would hover outside, peeping. If the stool had not landed in the passage, she would place it beside the bed. She would go to the cupboard and take down the cup and plate and hide them in the bed. She would take down the curtain pole. Fetch the soap, toothpaste, all her clothes. The clothes she would spread over the floor, arrange and rearrange them endlessly, over and over again.

They would keep up a continual watch, but she would notice nothing. She would sit on the bed, tearing her thinnest blouse into ribbons. Slowly, slowly shredding. She would bombard the first one to open the door with all she had hidden in the bed. The whole time she would chant, "just keep on turning--keep on turning--keep on turning," stare madly and roll her eyes.

No, that keep on turning bit wouldn't be good--too revealing, too close to the truth of the treatment here. She would sing the V signal, just as it was hammered out by the prisoners--on one note--always the same note.

She tried to sound out the most ear-splitting note and practiced her mad stare.

Suddenly she pulled up sharp: it would be wrong of her to pretend madness; time enough for the real thing. She could be glad that she had not already lost her reason. She cast her mind back, telling herself that she should be glad that things were as they were, now. She sat at the table and watched the clouds. From now on she would concentrate all her strength on blotting out the pain. Pain belonged to the body. She refused to let it destroy her soul. She refused to let it master her thoughts and feelings or to force her to sit lost in morbid self-pity. She prayed silently and whistled a few bars of a tune and soon life once again became more than mere existence.

Tralla was kind: one day she left the door open as her other neighbor was walking by. It was good to know what one's neighbors looked like. Until then, Tora had only known her footstep. Always quick and light, it reminded her of a skipping bird. A nervous glance and quick smile were all she could recall. A moving smile, so lonely and helpless. She too had been in solitary confinement for more than six months. Her name was Solveig.

Tora learned later that she too had been beaten. Her hearing had been all but destroyed. They were devils, Solveig said. Every one. Without exception. Devils. She hammered out the word, loud and strong. "You don't know them yet," she said. Tora couldn't answer. She felt that she knew her captors well enough; but Solveig had been imprisoned for so long. Tora asked her if she had work. The answer was encouraging: she had just been given a small amount of darning to do for the prisoners. She seemed excited. Well, one could undoubtedly get to the stage when one longed to be allowed to do some darning even though, for her own part, Tora felt that this would take a very long time.

That evening something unusual was going on in the courtyard. There was a roll call. Tora could see that the boys had a strange tenseness about them. Those who answered to their names appeared either downcast or else they grinned. She was at a loss to understand these grins for there was something in their eyes that did not add up. She asked Matti what was happening. "Deportation," was the brief reply.

Matti did not want to exchange signals that evening. Tora lay down. All was silent in the courtyard but she was unable to sleep. The boys had ceased to be anonymous prisoners: they were fathers--brothers--Harald. The following day she was exhausted and ashen-faced.

A few days later the prisoners were transported. She had been unaccountably downcast all day, but as the convoy of trucks rolled up, she began to understand why.

The prisoners emerged from the main entrance with their papers and baggage and wearing their own clothes. They lined up directly under her window.

The women warders kept a close watch on the cells. Funcke came in and, on finding Tora sitting at the table, left without comment. As soon as the sound of her footsteps had died away, Tora went to the window. Funcke was good like that: you could always hear her walk.

The boys appeared to be in high spirits. They joked about each other's clothes and tried on each other's caps and hats. With affected jollity, they measured suits that had become too large or assured one another cheerily: "It'll be good to get a change of routine, lads!" What a show they put on.

A couple of the boys were scuffling together. One glanced continually up at one of the windows as he struggled to get free. "Where was she? Why didn't she come?"

A young man stood close to the fence, apart from the others. She could see the deep mahogany shine of his hair in the evening sun. His face was grave. He stood motionless, gazing at the landscape, then turned his head as though to take it all in. He turned towards the fjord. Tora could see his back; the outline of the young body was confident and steadfast. He tilted his head back slightly and seemed to breathe in the land and air.

One old fellow was near to tears. He scrubbed at his eyes with gnarled, blue fingers. Those nearest him taunted and laughed, pulling at his skimpy trouser legs, jostling him back and forth. Someone pushed a cigarette into his mouth. And all the while, this horseplay cried out more clearly than words: "Pull yourself together, man!"

The man who had given him the cigarette turned, rubbed his chin for some time, pulled at his collar, coughed, turned towards somebody else and began to whistle.

Another was gnawing at a crust, chewing and chewing, long after there was nothing left to chew. His face was totally without expression.

A lad of about eighteen was evidently telling a good joke. His companion guffawed.

Suddenly an order for silence was barked out.

Near the steps, someone was packing his sack for the fourth time. He seemed not to know how to cram everything in. A red sweater, a shirt, two pairs of socks, a pair of underpants, and a parcel wrapped in newspaper. He had shaken out and refolded the underpants twice. He shook them out for the third time, rolled them up, and pushed them into a pocket.

One of the group stood looking at him--smoking, endlessly smoking, letting the butts fall where he stood and lighting up another cigarette. The man beside him picked up the butts, peeled off the paper and shook the tobacco into a grimy handkerchief.

Others made no attempt at pretense. They were leaving,

leaving their homeland, wives, and children. They knew what awaited them; and on that day and at that hour, they fully knew what they were leaving behind.

The last name was called and the prisoners were piled into trucks. As they rolled through the gates, Tora caught a fleeting glimpse of shining teeth clenched in an attempted smile and a handkerchief waving a forbidden farewell through a slit in the tarpaulin.

Dentzer and three officers came in through the gates. Dentzer had an air of relief about him. He rubbed his hands together; it was as though he had washed his hands of the disappearing convoy.

Tora lay looking at the stars. Thinking of wives and mothers. The stars grew pale before she slept.

Spring was in the air. Tora was arranging her cell which had been inspected while she had been absent during exercise. Garments were strewn about. They had been in the bed too this time. The stool had been moved and the blind cord was still swinging slowly; it had not occurred to her before that the blind could be used as a hiding place. She was sure that Black Maria had been on the prowl. She could tell from the smell and the chaos--the familiar traces of her brutal methods. Tora felt that she should be used to these inspections by now, but they distressed her as much as ever. It was worst when they had taken place without her being there. She could not explain it to herself; it was as though some treasured personal belonging had been destroyed.

With her belongings once more in order, she began to feel more at home and to turn her mind to the approach of spring. There were no visible signs; and yet it was there--a gentle, barely discernible undertone. Lately for supper they had been given a smear of butter and some kind of spread with the four slices of bread. One evening she was given a spoonful of black syrup; she felt the burnt taste on her tongue and it was good. She placed herself so that she could see the pale colors of the evening sky, while savoring each morsel. Butter, butter-- surely there was no taste so heavenly!

Her deliberate masticating stopped at the sound of a musi- cal note outside her window, the chirp of a lone bird. The same note, over and over again. What was it saying? "Just wait--just wait--just wait." The message was as clear as if it had been spoken. The prisoner smiled. Fair enough--she was used to waiting, she knew she would pull through.

Tora signaled to Matti. "Did you hear that bird?"

"Yes. It was here last year too."

Last year! My poor Apple Blossom. Her smile died away.

Solveig had not heard it. Tora told her about its message: just wait--just wait--just wait. Solveig made no comment on the bird but only asked Tora how long she thought the war would continue. "They say it will be over by Easter." She often asked the same question. Tora always answered yes, even though she herself did not believe it. Tora had been alarmed once when a girl to whom she had passed on some bad news had fallen ill; she had never told a disappointing truth since.

Of course the war would be over by Easter. Imagine, by Easter! Or at least by Whitsun. The time would fly by. Let's say Whitsun, to be on the safe side. We'll go to the mountains in the summer. Think of the mountains, Solveig!

Tora had no desire to speak of the war. She had no chance of knowing what was going on in the world outside. Events must take their course. It could last a long time. She lived in a world of never ending pain, where all her strength was taken by the day-to-day struggle for existence. To live for the day was the only way to survive, the only way to carry on unbro- ken by the tyranny of waiting, the only way to endure.

Eleven

One day, as Tora was sitting with her plate of glutinous green fish, Black Maria arrived and told her to put on her coat.

"Why?"

"A visitor," she said, rattling keys impatiently.

A visitor! If the ground had opened before her, Tora would have felt no greater surprise. A visitor--for her! She hobbled out with trembling knees, unable to think clearly. It must be her sister.

When they reached the little house by the roadside where visitors were received, she saw that it was indeed her sister, Gerda. She wept at the sight of Tora.

"Don't cry. We haven't time," Tora said. It was strange-- she felt absolutely nothing; her mind was a void. A German, together with the young boy who was the interpreter in Dentzer's office, stood watching them. A male prisoner was being visited at the same time by his wife and five-year-old son.

"Have you got the mumps?" Gerda worked in a doctor's office, and ran expert hands over her throat.

"Is it swollen? Have you got a mirror?"

The German guard kept a close watch on them. It was strange to see her own reflection after so many months. It was not an attractive sight; Tora barely recognized herself in the pale, bloated face.

"My throat doesn't hurt."

"Are you sure? What are your teeth like?" She grasped Tora's chin, opened her mouth and scrutinized her teeth as thoroughly as a farmer at a horse fair. She must stop this before she gets thrown out or arrested, Tora thought, as she saw the German guard approaching. The girl is mad.

"Show me your nails--are you suffering from a vitamin deficiency?" She examined the prisoner's hands. The guard was standing close beside her. Tora was faint with fear.

"I'll give you some Vitamin C," Gerda said, taking up a parcel and opening it.

"That's not allowed. The prisoners get medical and dental treatment and all the medicines they need." The guard spoke in broken Norwegian. Tora was tempted to say that this was not true, but dared not for the sake of her sister.

The guard checked the parcel. A few cigarette packs lay tantalizingly near. "Absolutely forbidden!" Tora fixed her gaze on a large jar of strawberries which was also placed in the pile of forbidden fruits.

The male prisoner began to cry, and suddenly, Gerda's parcel was no longer of interest. He sat with his head in his hands--weeping silently--silently. His wife sat beside him, pale and distressed. Tora wanted to cry out: "Why don't you embrace him? Take him in your arms! Kiss him! Stroke his hair! Don't you understand his desperate loneliness? Let him feel a body close to his own!"

As from far away, she heard Gerda telling her that all was well at home. Her landlady had asked to be remembered to her. Recalling herself suddenly, Tora asked her sister if she had taken care of the paint box, and had she managed to eat the cakes in the bread bin before they were mildewed? The guard looked at the weeping prisoner. "Thirty days on bread and water," Tora whispered, noisily crumpling the paper from the parcel. She wondered if Gerda had understood the remark about the cakes. Raising her voice, she said that she had borrowed some kitchen things from Anna, including the bread bin. Would Gerda be so kind as to return them?

"You don't need to worry about the kitchen things. Everything has been arranged in the best possible way. Anna is married now and she's very well."

The time was up and Grandma came to fetch her. Tora parted from Gerda in a daze.

"Everything has been arranged in the best possible way." The words echoed in her head. So, Marit and Gerda had arranged it all--just as she had thought. Even more reason to keep silent.

The reaction that engulfed her after the visit was so strong that her whole body shook. She was unable to eat the fish. Unable to walk. She sat thinking of all the things she should have asked about. Her longing for her family had suddenly been laid bare, a reopened wound. She had not dared to ask about Harald. She had feared the guard; they were always more suspicious when a man was involved. She could still not understand why she had been allowed to have a visitor and was convinced that it had come about because of a misunderstanding. Whatever the reason, she blessed the day and, in spite of the pain and restlessness the meeting had caused, she hoped for more.

She could not get the male prisoner out of her mind. The lifeless grey tinge of his hair had reminded her of the boy who had been with her on the journey to Grini. She knew that the prisoner was at that moment sitting in his cell crying, his loneliness intensified by the recent meeting. She wanted no more visits; they made loneliness even more unbearable.

The smell of a grocery store hung about the parcel--and the scent of oranges. Tora spread the small packets over the table and gave herself over to the sweet pleasures of sight and smell before beginning to taste. She moved the two oranges closer to the green wall and rearranged a small piece of cheese. It was so more in harmony with the lines of the table top.

She picked up an orange. Her fingers traced its shape, felt the uneven surface. The sun-gold skin breathed life. She put it back on the table and gazed--and gazed; this was what she wanted it to be--a thing of beauty to look upon.

In the evening she divided the packet of butter and roll of sweets into three. Matti signaled thanks: "It was wonderful to find something on the wall. A miracle that Black Maria didn't smell the orange!" Tora's share had disappeared long before she went to bed.

The remaining half of the orange lay in the cupboard, giving off a faint smell. Tora lay thinking about it. Solveig should have it. She turned over towards the wall. Yes, she would give it to Solveig. She awoke in the middle of the night and smelled the tantalizing fragrance. No--it was for Solveig! Several days passed before an opportunity to pass on the small gifts presented itself; but eventually Solveig was knocking out rapturous thanks--for one quarter of an orange and two or three sweets--to a conscience-stricken Tora on the other side of the wall.

The days ran on. The only diversion was provided by the knocking and the joyous song of the bird: "Just wait--just wait --just wait." Tora had grown to love the bird; in her imagination she saw it, perched high up in a leafless birch, swelling out its tiny breast and cocking its head. And there was the refrain: "Just wait--just wait--just wait." No day was complete without the sound of the bright song.

It was Easter Eve. The prisoners were not taken out for exercise; the guards were too busy distributing parcels. The corridor was alive with sound. Freyer's room lay opposite Tora's cell and she could hear each time the door was opened and closed. There were sounds of unfamiliar footsteps, rattling boxes, and crackling paper, and an occasional thud when someone arrived with a new load of parcels and dropped them onto the floor.

Freyer and Grandma were checking the parcels, with Funcke and Black Maria probably distributing them to various cells. Tora could hear the joyous whoops of the prisoners when the doors were unlocked. Those from the open section were apparently allowed to fetch their own parcels; the unfamiliar footsteps must be theirs. Tora hoped that the prisoner with the sad eyes would get many parcels; perhaps then she would smile. The girl with the shiny, bobbed hair was sure to get several. Tora shook her head and smiled at her own thoughts and reactions--locked in isolation, growing fond of totally unknown people.

Solveig had a parcel. Matti had two. Whenever footsteps approached her door, Tora was sure that it was Funcke coming with her parcel. Of course they had sent a parcel--all of them at home--a small, joint parcel. And Marit would have sent something. Maybe others too. Marit for sure.

Tora did not expect to hear from Harald. He might be in England. She knew that she would hear no more from him until after the war. This she accepted. One day they would meet--of this she was sure.

The days passed. Tora's door was unlocked many times, but there was no parcel. She walked the cell, telling herself that it didn't matter, it wasn't that they hadn't wanted to. None of them had forgotten her. That she could not believe. No--she knew that they were thinking of her--every day. Maybe this was yet another part of her punishment. It could just be that the parcel was delayed. She whistled a jaunty tune.

Jumping at a slight sound behind her, she saw a large slab of chocolate lying under the ventilation shaft by the door. Real chocolate!

She hardly dared to reach out for it--or indeed to believe that it was real. She pressed herself close to the wall by the sink, where she could not be seen from outside, and examined the wrapper. It gave no clue. She sniffed at the chocolate and broke off a piece. It was then that she discovered something scratched onto it: "Happy Easter! Lolo." Who was Lolo? Imagine, a whole chocolate bar! A prewar chocolate bar! Unknown kind Lolo--how kind you are to think of a prisoner you don't even know! And just when I was feeling so alone-- forgotten by everyone. Can you understand how happy you have made me? Can you understand that your generosity has given me more happiness that all the parcels in the world?

There was more to come. The shaft was a veritable cornucopia: two pieces of white bread and a paper napkin wrapped round six biscuits thickly spread with butter. In a corner of one of the napkins there was a small picture of an Easter chicken--yellow, jaunty. Tora hid it away. Black Maria shouldn't get her claws into it. She walked twice round the cell and then took out the napkin and looked at the chicken. Solveig was knocking. "We're going to send you something good just as soon as we get a chance. Keep an eye on the top of the wall." After the evening round she found a packet. It contained cake--a large slice, delicious, feathery-light, some slices of sausage--unbelievable! And a small dab of butter--she could feel the smooth taste already running in her mouth, two fingers of baking chocolate and two or three boiled sweets.

Tora felt no shame as she cried tears of joy and gratitude; for all this luxury Matti could have kept to herself and enjoyed alone.

Later that evening Matti told her that she had on several occasions asked if she could have a Bible. Other reading material she could have, but no Bible, nor any of the the text books she would need if she were to be able to continue with her studies. Tora could offer no explanation why she was not allowed to have school books. As for the Bible, perhaps they feared that reading it might bring on some sort of mental crisis, she had been alone for so long. Matti broke in abruptly: "It's Dentzer who refuses. He says the Bible is a book of fairy tales for Jews." She wanted to know what Tora thought about God and religion in general. Tora asked her to wait until the following day. She was exhausted from the emotional aftermath of the day's events; to be able to speak of that faith which for her was life itself, she would have to be wide awake and rested.

She lay for a long time thinking back over her long search for God, back to the time of her confirmation. She recalled the disappointment of many questions unanswered by priest and teachers, questions brushed aside or avoided. There had been much talk of blood and salvation, of God's eternal punishment, of the life hereafter, with garlands and crowns for the faithful, a heaven of harps and palms. She had found no God in their talk, or in their lives. Those who had called themselves Christians-- they had no love for each other. There was no sharing. No kindness, no goodness, no solicitude, no tolerance. Instead, the young seeker of God had met narrow-minded fanatics, arrogant and joyless.

Later, she had found her path obscured by the very teachings of the church. What was the Trinity? Who was God? God--or Christ? Neither had she found her God in the great churches. At last she had begun to read Swedenborg; and gradually the biblical interpretations of the old Swedish scientist had opened the way to God--to that God she had always sought to love--to Christ as God. And so, as she lay, she looked forward to discussing all these things with Matti on the following day. Her faith was a safe haven where she could find security in her life, and she knew that without her strength in the Lord she could not have endured the oppressions of the past months.

Streaks of dawn were already in the sky when she fell asleep with thanksgiving on her lips.

When the wind was in the right direction, she could hear the church bells on Sunday mornings. She loved the good sound. It brought peace. There was porridge for dinner. Sugar too--a whole spoonful. It was the first time she had seen sugar during her time in prison. She wanted to lift the plate and lick it clean even though she knew that no morsel could have escaped her meticulous scraping. She gave the spoon a final lick, lifted the plate up once more and closely examined the table. She might still have overlooked something! The first time she had lifted the plate she had discovered two grains of sugar. She had quite forgotten the intense sweetness of its taste.

All that afternoon she signaled to Matti through the wall, explaining briefly her ideas and beliefs about God and religion. She spoke to her about the teachings of The New Church and of all her old uncertainties which had fallen so naturally into place. Matti's only answer was that she had never looked at things in that way.

About a month later Tora received a second visit. It was just as unexpected as the first and all she had intended to ask about was once more forgotten. She had seen two yellow coltsfoot blooming by the roadside and had hastily picked them. She showed them happily to her sister. "Yes, things are going the right way now--the days are getting lighter and lighter. Soon it will be summer."

Tora asked once if the bread bin had been returned, and was reassured that everything to do with the kitchen had been seen to. At last she felt safe: everything was in order.

On this occasion she was not allowed to take her parcel with her; it would be brought up later by the interpreter.

The parting from her sister was painful--worse than the last time. She looked back and waved. Black Maria shoved her forward--such behavior was strictly forbidden.

Tora straightened her shoulders, lifted her head, and smiled at a group of male prisoners they passed. They were not allowed to return her smile. They were not allowed to see her. They were allowed to stand to attention for Black Maria; but Tora knew that it was for her they did so. As she passed Matti's cell, she placed a coltsfoot on the stool outside the door.

A few hours later Freyer and Dentzer appeared. Tora could hear before the door was unlocked that Dentzer was in a fighting mood.

She was gripped by sudden anxiety for her sister. Had the interpreter guessed something? Dear God, don't let her be taken in!

The sight of Dentzer reassured her: he was there for something quite different. He came straight into the cell and immediately began to shout at her. His face was flushed with anger and his eyes wild. The hard voice beat about her head; she felt as though it would split in two. "What's been going on? Communist pig--you've been allowed to see a visitor! Twice even! You, who shouldn't see another living soul!" He drew a breath, giving Tora a chance to protest that she wasn't the one who arranged the visits and to ask in surprise why should she not be allowed to have visitors in the same way as the other prisoners.

There was a murderous look in his eyes. He continued to rage, saying this was the last time she would see her sister alive. The visit had come about through a misunderstanding at The Terrace.

He suddenly became calmer, motioned Freyer in from where she had been standing in the doorway with the parcel, and concluded by saying in a mild tone that on this occasion he would temper justice with mercy and allow her to keep the parcel--if she would only talk.

There was nothing to say that had not already been said. Tora turned her back and started her customary round. He remained standing. He cracked the riding whip in his hand against his boot. "Well?" The tone was threatening. Tora stopped in front of him and asked when she would be able to see the dentist. A look as though he longed to strangle her passed over his face. He turned on his heel with clinking spurs and slammed the door behind him.

For some time following this incident she was tormented by anxiety for her sister. She listened fearfully to the voice and footfall of every new prisoner. Nothing happened and the tension slowly subsided. She was not summoned for further questioning.

Matti spoke of her brother in solitary confinement at

Akershus Fortress. Another was probably in Sweden. Their father was a prisoner of war somewhere abroad.

Two children locked up alone in two of the most notorious prisons in the country; a second hunted like an animal; her husband a prisoner in a foreign country. Tora had grown to love Matti's mother. She had become a symbol for her, the embodiment of the best in people. Matti said that she never complained, was never concerned for herself. In her thoughts Tora lived close to her through the days--and nights. Dear Lord, help Matti's mother.

There was something wrong with Solveig. A menacing silence hung about her cell. Tora signaled, but there was no reply. She tried once or twice during the day, not daring to knock too often for she was afraid that the girl was sick and that the noise would irritate her. She was restless at night. Maybe Solveig was feverish. She imagined her flushed face on the pillow. Frightening possibilities loomed up in her mind. Oh God, you must help!

Her first thoughts on waking were of Solveig. Tora knocked softly. There was no answer. Later in the day Freyer and a strange man went into the cell. Tora strained to hear. Was it the doctor? They stood afterwards talking in the passage. She was only able to make out the words "lying down."

There was no answering knock from Solveig for several days. She was not taken out for exercise nor did she go to fetch hot water in the evening. Matti asked every day if there was any change. Tora knocked cautiously in the morning, at midday, and in the evening, signaling that they understood and were thinking of her.

The suspense was eased slightly one day when Solveig tapped out a faint reply. Her messages were so puzzling at first that it seemed that she must be delirious; but her gradual improvement each day was marked by stronger, steadier signals.

Eventually she was able to tell them what had happened. She had fainted in the compound, injuring her head in the fall. Since then she had lain in bed, remembering nothing.

It was not the first time. She fainted often. Nothing was done about it. She lay where she fell until she regained consciousness. The worst was that she frequently hit her head so badly that she had to keep to her bed for several days after.

Tora thought at first that she had misunderstood the knocking. "Have they actually seen you lying after a fall and given you no help--done nothing--just let you lie there where you fell?" "Yes, the devils. They are devils--all of them!"

Tora wept as she struggled in vain to understand her fellow beings. She signaled to her other neighbor. All was not well with Matti: she was in a dilemma. When she heard of how Solveig had been treated, and saw how the young men were hounded, she was tempted to hate. And yet her captors were kind to her; it was not possible for her to summon up hate when such treatment had never been meted out to her.

It was good, Tora said, that Matti was unable to bring herself to hate; there were thousands who did. She said she was glad that they were kind to Matti because then she, Tora, could also find something that she could like them for.

She refrained from telling her young neighbor that the way she was treated had little to do with true kindness. She did not say that if she had been older, if it had not been for her captivating youthful appearance, she would have received precious little kindness. She did not say that this kindness was nothing more than cloying sentimentality.

Matti had her share of difficulties as it was. Tora knew that she was disliked by several of the prisoners because of her youth and beauty, and the fact that Dentzer and Freyer were kind to her. Poor Apple Blossom--there was nothing she could do about it. She was a good girl; her life would in no way be improved if she were filled with hate; nor would it bring about any change in either Dentzer or Freyer.

They doubtless glowed with self-righteousness after one of their short visits to Matti. Sometimes they gave her a cake or a cigarette, or admired her work; and they always left her with a clear conscience. Tora imagined that these visits acted as some sort of stabilizer, calming the storm--at least for the next cell they visited or the next prisoner to be interrogated by Dentzer.

The shadow of a smile given to Matti by a warder sometimes fell upon Tora, a faint, painful shadow: the hostility shown to her was in sharp contrast to the friendliness sometimes shown to others. She could not help envying Matti--but only for these smiles.

Little Matti--she had no idea of her corrective role in Tora's lonely existence.

Twelve

Outside it was spring. The parade ground was grey and muddy and the stretch between the main building and the electric fence was already green. Scattered coltsfoot bloomed cheerfully here and there. The distant meadows glowed in rich brown and evening purple. Now they had been planted and sown and potatoes already set in long rows. In front of the yellow house the birches were veiled with green.

Tora longed to paint. She asked Freyer if she could write off for materials.

"That's up to Dentzer to decide," she replied. He appeared one day in an affable mood. "Well, well--so the prisoner feels like doing some work at last. And what would she like to do?" Tora could hardly believe her ears, so agreeable was the tone. She needed pencils and paints, she said; she would so much like to draw and paint; could she write away for what she needed?

He smiled at her benevolently. So she had decided to talk at last? A raised brow and questioning look were her only reply.

There was an instant change. He seemed to swell. He swore and snarled: then she could sit there waiting for paper and paints until she rotted. This was the familiar tone--and the resounding slam of the door.

She was continually cold, even though she walked the cell all day long. Today it was raining. She loved the rain. She went to the window and looked out over the landscape. It lay soft under the showers, rolling away in endless shades of grey.

The prisoners working outside looked miserable. The tempo was unusually fast. Some were sullen and moved about with their heads drawn down as far as possible between their shoulders. They don't know how lucky they are, to be able to move about in the clear spring air and feel the rain on their faces. She would have smiled if she had been out there, smiled and raised her face to the rain.

There was no reply when she signaled to Matti in the evening. She lay on her bed, disappointed and uneasy.

Had she said something wrong, something that had hurt her? It wasn't always easy, signaling through the wall. Sometimes she forgot how young Matti was and that she had been kept alone for so long.

Was she ill? Dear Lord, don't let her be ill--and help her with her struggle.

Maybe it was the weather? Tora lay looking at the leaden sky, listening to the falling rain. She was wide awake and disconsolate. Maybe Matti lay crying?

The prisoners from the open section were showering in the basement. They chattered and laughed and shrieked. Snatches of words and melodies from jazz and hymns floated up through the walls.

Tora often sensed a hysterical undercurrent to the violent merriment. It was uncontrolled and filled with--filled with what? It could not be defined; but there was something that she disliked. She would pull herself up, telling herself that she was too critical, or that she felt that way because she was always alone, with no one to laugh with.

Yet she knew that all was not as it should be with the laughter and the voices. She was familiar with several of the voices, but not the owners.

On this particular evening she was irritated, and the droll remarks and singing afforded no amusement. It was no more than a cacophony of out-of-tune screeches and yells, and there was a meanness in the raucous laughter--while Matti lay suffering, crying. She was sure that Matti was crying.

After the open prisoners had clattered up the stairs and all was silent once more, she heard the sound of lonely, painful sobbing, coming through the wall from Matti's cell.

The desolation.... "Matti, Matti--." Tora leaned against the wall and passed her hand over it slowly, not daring to knock. The sounds grew louder. A vision of Matti rose before her, gasping, her small figure shaken by wave after wave of un-controllable sobbing.

Tora lay down again. She was cold. The pain--the pain. "Matti--Matti dear--don't cry--you're not alone, you know-- don't cry, Matti."

There was no Whitsuntide parcel for Tora; this she had almost expected. It didn't matter. Not any longer, now that she knew the reason why.

Matti shared the contents of hers. She always shared; and Tora accepted with joy and gratitude, knowing that she would never be able to return this generosity.

Two days later Dentzer came, with Freyer at his heels. He was carrying a large parcel. He told her who the parcel was from and proceeded to lift out each item and show it to her.

A large packet of butter, a piece of cheese, a cake, a tub of marmalade, a chocolate bar, a piece of sausage and, finally, five packs of cigarettes. The prisoner played the interested onlooker, occasionally commenting--"mmm" and "lovely!" She smiled at Dentzer as he slowly, slowly replaced the cigarettes.

She was prepared for what was to come. He straightened up and looked at her coaxingly. It was too sad that she should have to while her time away in boredom. She was no more than an innocent tool in the hands of the ringleaders. How would she like to be moved to the open section, together with the others? Yes, that would be wonderful--the prisoner thought. She studied his face. He could guarantee that she would be moved to the open section, get her parcel, and be permitted to receive all subsequent parcels. She would be allowed to write, read, and work in the same way as the others, or take drawing materials outside and work with them there. How was the tooth? Still aching? The dentist would look at it tomorrow. She could see the doctor, if and whenever necessary. She would be allowed to smoke as much as she liked--if she would only--well, let's see--he had no wish to be too demanding--all this should be hers if she would only reveal the name of that one contact, the one with the money. All the rest would be forgotten.

After all, she was not a Communist--so what then was the point of shielding this contact? He looked at her questioningly. She looked back, not answering.

He cleared his throat. He could stretch himself even further. Her behavior as a prisoner had been exemplary. If she would give him the information he wanted now, he would arrange with the Gestapo for her to be set free within a month. Completely free! A wonderful offer! Now--what about it? Tora thought of the life she was willing to give for the freedom of the land, for those working on in the world outside, and was suddenly overcome with a hysterical urge to laugh--laugh right in his face.

She contented herself with a smile, a candid gaze. It was sad, but there was nothing more she could tell.

"Will not, you mean!" Freyer snarled. Tora was never quite able to forgive her for those words.

It was summer and Tora was happy. It was an unusually pleasant day, beginning with Funcke smiling at her as she unlocked for the morning rounds--a genuine smile which warmed her so that she wanted to throw her arms around the stiff, unbending Funcke. The prisoner smiled at the thought of the reaction this would have brought about. The woman would have instantly been on the defense, thinking that she was being attacked. Tora felt the warmth of the smile all morning.

Then there was the pleasure of the flower, a small scarlet button just outside the netting fence of the exercise compound. She had been watching the bud for several days, anticipating its unfolding.

The first thing she saw that day as she entered the compound was the red flower. She stood still and looked and looked--until she heard a shout of "Keep going!" from the watch tower.

She took the flower with her, her conscience pricking as she thought of the other prisoners who would be cheered by the sight of it; but there were many buds and soon there would be many scarlet flowers.

At first she placed it carefully in the sink; but there it was hidden so she stuck it jauntily into a cleaned-out toothpaste tube. She wasn't quite sure where she wanted it--in the middle of the scrubbed table or nearer the wall. She moved it, took a couple of paces back, deliberated, and moved it once more. That's where it looked best, nearer the wall, the red so good against the green. Her spirits lifted. That was just what was needed, that little touch of scarlet, of warmth. It gave life both to the table and to the wall.

On the fourth day when she came up from the compound the flower had disappeared. She raged, hammering on the door with clenched fists and boot heels.

Black Maria approached with leaden steps from the other end of the corridor.

"Who has taken my flower?"

Black Maria pulled the door to with a clang. "Halle's round the bend. Ever heard such nonsense? And all over a dead weed in that tin contraption. We must keep some sort of order in the cells."

Tora was apprehensive--fearful for Matti--afraid that something was going to happen to her. As she had passed her cell on the midday round she had seen Dentzer and Freyer standing outside. Dentzer had not noticed her. They were talking about Matti. He was looking thoughtfully at the closed door. She had been sent for a medical examination. Tora felt a vague unease, a presentiment of Germany in the air. They had started sending women down now--fifteen in the last consignment. She had stood bereft, watching a dark, bobbed head disappear into a van.

She said nothing to Matti about the incident in the corridor; but signaled to her a little more often.

Matti was irritated by the persistent knocking. She had no wish to drop the animals she was busily making to listen to Tora rambling on about Matti's apple blossom complexion and brown eyes flecked with green!

Tora stood close to the wall for a moment, wishing that she could push it in over Matti. Then she took up her walking once more. This was nothing to cry over. Of course it was more fun for Matti to carry on with her work. It was the wall between that prevented her from understanding. And Matti could have no idea of what it was like to be shut up with nothing to do. It was she herself who was thoughtless: of course it was irritating to have to break off from a beautiful, floppy-eared dog just as one was trying to work out where the tail should be placed.

If only Solveig had been able to hear better. It wasn't always easy: often when Tora had laboriously hammered out some important piece of news Solveig would answer "yes"--only to ask two seconds later if she had heard any news. At such times Tora couldn't be bothered to signal any more.

Tora drifted around with her hands behind her back, imagining what her toy dog would look like, if she had been allowed to make one. At least it would not be a German shepherd! Dentzer owned a huge beast with watchful eyes. She would make a beagle, with contours to its body, soft dangling ears and kind, sorrowful eyes. No doubt it would be a droll creature--but kind: it would never attack a prisoner.

On the following day, Matti had great news. The wall vibrated with her knocking. "Freyer has said that I'm not going to be on my own any longer. I'm going to be moved in with you!" Tora held her breath and asked Matti to repeat the end of the signal. "With you, yes! Freyer and Dentzer were standing outside here this morning. I pushed the disc to one side and listened. They were discussing you while you were out in the compound. Freyer suggested moving you in here-- she said we belong together in any case. Perhaps they've heard us knocking. I couldn't quite get what Dentzer said, but it was something about Communism." "Are you a Communist?" "No, but he thinks I am."

Tora lay awake with hammering heart. If she could only move in with Matti and really get to look at the apple blossom skin, the green-flecked eyes, the jaunty checked skirt. She had never quite been able to see the rest of Matti's face. And to be able to speak again! Not to have the wall between them when Matti was sick with depression and longing. Maybe she could help her through these times. She could try to get her to think of others things, to laugh even. And if that didn't work, she would remind her of her mother. And yet that might make things even worse for Matti? No--not if she trod warily.

From time to time, when Tora was tempted to succumb to self-pity, her thoughts would turn to Matti's mother; then her spirits would rise once more and she would feel shame and gratitude.

So, Dentzer had spoken of Communism. She lay and tried to sort out in her mind why she could never be a Communist. A political conviction could never be her religion, a party could never be her god. As long as Communism used hate for its ends, and denied the existence of the god of freedom and love, it would be impossible for her to join its ranks.

For some days Matti and Tora lived in happy anticipation of the impending change, signaling to each other of pleasures to come.

Tora would be able to work--of course. Together they would make animals and birds and dolls, and read and have discussions, and tell jokes and relive amusing experiences. They would even work out a daily exercise routine.

There was a change, but not for Tora. She struggled through the ensuing days, telling herself that it was good for Matti--very good. Kari would be better company for Matti than she could ever have been.

Kari was sweet. Kari was good. It wasn't her fault that she had been placed with Matti instead of her.

She was so cheerful too. Matti could have no better companion.

And they had a wonderful time together. Their laughter came rippling through the wall. They did all the things that she and Matti had planned.

Tora tried to smile when the laughter rose at its highest. She wasn't too successful--and then she reproached herself and told herself that she should be glad--glad for Matti's sake. Things were so much better for her now. It was good that she had Kari for company. Kari, who was so kind.

And it was quite understandable that Matti no longer had time to signal to her as often as before. Yes--it was natural, only to be expected, quite natural, and yet....

Stop that! It wasn't that the girl no longer wanted to. And even if she didn't, that was nothing to sulk over. It was reasonable. Of course it was more fun to talk than to have to communicate by a laborious system of knocking. And it must be irritating to listen to, particularly since she was no longer taking part in the knocking herself.

And imagine how happy Matti's mother would be when she knew that Matti had company. Truly congenial company. She had to stop being envious and try instead to share in their happiness.

It was difficult, and it took time; but she was eventually able to take part. She smiled when they laughed and was amused by their gymnastics. Kari was learning to stand on her hands; but if the sound of her falls were anything to go by, she had all the lightness and grace of a well grown hippo. And for Tora, the laughter that followed each tumble slowly grew to be a veritable elixir of life.

Thirteen

One afternoon Tralla swept in and told her to pack. "Quickly! Quickly!" Her mind was frozen as she gathered her few garments together. The only thought in her mind was that she must say goodbye to those in the neighboring cell. It was not possible. Tralla stood in the doorway nagging.

It wasn't true. She knew that it wasn't true, that it wouldn't last. She did not bother to unpack her things.

She had been placed in a large cell with five other prisoners. As in a dream she gazed from one to the other, absorbing each new voice and breathing in the atmosphere of living beings.

She sat telling them about the interrogations and thinking of how wonderful it was. If only the others knew how it felt! She was so overjoyed that she longed to embrace them all.

The thought of returning to isolation was unendurable. She could stand no more. She hungered for human company.

She talked and talked, devouring impressions. One of her new companions shared a chocolate bar, giving Tora the largest piece. There was a sweetness about her, a warmth, and an impression of motherliness. Tora was touched and thanked her, at the same time feeling a longing to ask if she could instead hold her hands, lay her head in her lap, and wash away some of her loneliness with tears. Six months alone? How had she managed to survive, they wondered. "It wasn't too bad, it wasn't too bad," she replied, listening for the footsteps she was certain would come.

After a couple of hours she heard them approaching. Freyer stood there, looking grim and angry, with Tralla hovering nervously in the background.

She was not going! She refused to go back to desolation. God, why were they playing this cat-and-mouse game with her? She wanted to throw herself to the floor, kick, scream, refuse to go. She wanted to hide behind the others and cry: "Don't let them take me! Help me! I'll go mad if I have to go back to that loneliness."

They stood silently. Tora could feel the tears flooding their hearts. Freyer told her to move. She felt a wild desire to hit her, to knock her down. Instead, she said goodbye to the others. Her last glimpse of them was blurred, her smile of farewell trembling.

The sound of the footsteps behind her made her straighten her shoulders and lift her head. She refused to let them see that they were slowly killing her. Let them believe that she could stand it all. She smiled at Freyer as she let her into the cell; not her old cell with the view of the spruces and the yellow house, with Solveig and Kari and Matti as neighbors, but the one on the other side of the corridor.

She carefully put down her bundle of clothes. Freyer stood outside for a few moments, peeping. She wasn't going to let her see that she longed to tear down the bed, smash the window, and hurl the stool against the door.

Tora began to pace round the cell. "Pull yourself together, pull yourself together, pull yourself together--." She stepped out, timing her strides to the words and summoning all her strength and determination to keep going until the time when she could lie down.

From here there was no starlit heaven to look upon; she stared dry-eyed into a grey wall. The window was nailed fast and the panes painted over. Darkness was everywhere. The bunk above her head seemed to press down on her. She was unable to sleep and lay staring into a void.

During the day she walked the cell, without thoughts, without feelings, without living. At night she lay staring into the darkness, hardly knowing if she slept or was awake. All will to live was gone. The mound of dry bread in the cupboard grew and grew.

Tralla was unhappy. She pointed at the two bunks and said that soon Tora would be getting company. Tora looked at her. She knew that the woman was deliberately lying to console her. She smiled at her, meaning to say "It doesn't matter. Nothing matters any longer." And the pile of bread grew and grew.

After one week she was moved back to her old cell. Trembling and eager, she signaled to Matti and Kari. There was no reply. She knew they were there; she could hear their laughter and recognized their voices.

Matti can't have forgotten the signals? She knocked again. The laughter died away but there was no reply. They must reply! They were the only souls left on earth. They cannot have forgotten her. She spelled out her name. A reply was slowly hammered out: "We thought you had been moved in with the others." She walked away from the wall.

It was clear that they were not pleased to have her back. "We thought you had been moved in with the others." "So that's what you thought. That's how much you have missed me. That's how much you've thought about me. You thought I had been moved in with the others." There was a chill undertone in the messages, a distant, icy chill.

What a welcome! After the hell of the other cell. She wished they knew what she had been through. Egoists! She made up her mind not to signal any more.

Why couldn't they have at least pretended--welcomed her so that she could have walked up and down her cell, safe in the illusion that they were happy to have her back? Now she had no one. There was not a soul who cared for her, no one on earth who missed her.

She heard knocking on Matti's wall. She did not reply. They need not bother--she would trouble them no more. She needed no sympathy. She couldn't stand sympathy. She wanted love.

Keep on knocking--you can carry on until judgement day --I want none of your sympathy--do you hear? Stop it! You're only putting it on. What is sympathy worth anyway? It's all a worthless fake. I need none of it--I can manage alone. Alone? What about God? No, she did not want to think about God.

For a couple of days she withdrew entirely into herself. She made no reply to the signaling. Isolation she could overcome; but a loneliness devoid of any life, that she could not survive. As on so many occasions in the past, her thoughts turned to God. Slowly and painfully, grappling with the realization of her foolishness, her selfishness and lack of love, she managed to throw off the overwhelming mood of despondency. She was sitting with her hand against the wall, wondering how she should start, when a note fluttered down through the hole in the door. When she had read the note, it was even more difficult for her to begin.

She was moved. They had been glad for her, imagining her happily settled with the others. They had had no idea that she was isolated once more on the other side of the passage. A stranger had been placed in her cell when she was away. That was why they had not answered. They had been astonished when she came back. Why had she not answered? Was she not well? She read the closing words several times. "Welcome back, Tora. It is so good to have you here once more." She cried softly. Once again, life was worth living.

Her days were now tolerable and yet she remained depressed. The aftermath of the recent events was long lasting: she was unable to forget her stay with the others and in reliving the experiences of that brief spell, the pain of renewed isolation was intensified.

The warders were more brutal than ever--ill-tempered, spiteful, hounding and scolding without ceasing. She felt increasingly oppressed, physically and mentally. She flinched at the sound of Funcke's shout--"Faster! Faster!" She sensed a growing terror of the 'Mountain of Meat'; she was never safe from her. She trembled when she sensed that somebody was looking at her through the hole in the cell door, and had the feeling that her oppressors were taking advantage of her fears. They terrorized her in quite a different way from before.

Realizing that something would have to be done if she were to survive, she hit on what at the outset seemed to be a brilliant idea. She had a cigarette which she had been hiding for a long time. The constant, round-the-clock checks had prevented her from smoking it. She would light it under their noses, in the middle of the afternoon. She would show them that she wasn't frightened--she couldn't be intimidated so easily.

It was no great matter: she would not be endangering others. She could have found the cigarette on the way to the compound; the open prisoners were allowed to smoke--one of them could have easily dropped it. She still had the match and scrap of sandpaper from the night of the interrogation at The Terrace. She divided the sandpaper into two; she would hand over the smallest piece if she were discovered. It was all arranged. She only had to convince herself and her captors that she would not be broken.

She sat up on the bed and slowly lit the cigarette. With heart pounding and sweat pouring, she inhaled and smoked slowly, very slowly. Never before had a cigarette given her so little pleasure.

There was a hammering on the door from the men's section. Tora's hand began to shake.

Funcke came from the far end of the passage and opened up. She could hear Dentzer's voice thundering.

Tora felt an urge to put out the cigarette, wave the smoke away, wash herself and drink water. Instead, she compelled herself to remain seated, listening to the sound of the approaching footsteps. She tapped ash carelessly onto the floor and mopped her brow with her free hand. As the sound of the steps passed by and retreated into the distance, she felt the cigarette stub burning her fingers.

So, it was finished--at last. She was overcome by relief and total exhaustion. She had been fortunate too: nobody came to the cell before the evening. She had won. Later she smiled at herself: the episode was reminiscent of a teenage revolt; but it had served its purpose: her strength of will was unbroken.

The toothache worsened. The pain bored through her eye and far into the brain; there was no escape from its torment. One day as she was standing at the window, gazing out in an attempt to forget the pain, she recognized among the prisoners on the parade ground, a man from her home town. Although she knew him by name only, she had a sudden feeling of being close to her own family. If he would only look up! Eventually he looked her way, seeming unsure at first and then recognizing her. His expression became suddenly grave; he drew himself up and stood at attention--as though the national anthem were being played, thought Tora. She looked about cautiously to see why he was standing at attention. There were no officers about, nor was he looking in the direction of Dentzer's office.

Henry, I know you are looking up at me. It is as though you are trying to say "I'm sorry that you are shut up in there while I can be out in sun and rain." Henry, you mustn't look so gallant--or I shall begin to cry.

At length he removed his cap and bowed respectfully in her direction. She turned away from the window.

Slowly she clawed her way up through the mire of depression. It helped her to think of those whose situation was worse than hers. There were more than enough to keep her thoughts occupied.

Often as she lay awake at night, racked by the pain of her tooth, she heard the sound of screams and blows from the men's section. It was impossible to get used to the sound of a lashing whip and the ensuing screams; but at such moments her own pain was forgotten.

Tora was sitting at the table, intently following the movements of a spider spinning its way up and down. She had grown fond of the small creature. It would appear from time to time, disappear, and then turn up once more. It was no beauty, but rare, and seemed to carry a caricature of a well-known politician on its silvery-grey and black back.

It seemed to appear for the sole purpose of amusing her, creeping always to the corner where she was sitting and drawing itself up and down, up and down. The small legs twitched with lightning activity and the gossamer thread quivered and swung, but never broke. She spoke to the spider, asked it if it knew where Harald was. The spider only spun and spun. If she had not seen it for several days she would send out an SOS through the wall. It often went over to Matti. Tora asked her to send it home again.

She was also visited by a bee and a small fly. The bee survived in captivity for about three hours. It didn't like it at all. It landed at last on the metal window hasp and, for a while, seemed to suck at it as though it imagined it to be a flower. Tora thought it was poisoned. In any event, it died.

The fly darted about the cell, examining everything but not finding even one small grain of sugar on which to land. It was no place for a fly. It struggled to find the way out, hit the windowpane a few times and fell, but was just as lively. It found an opening at last and disappeared. She didn't care much for flies, but preferred the bee that had died all because of a misunderstanding.

How long were they going to let him stand there in the blistering heat of the sun? He stood to attention, facing the office block. A placard hung on his chest but she could not make out the inscription. The other prisoners passed him by, unheeding.

He had been standing there for hours. Every time he slumped or moved a foot, a command was yelled from one of the offices. The placard blew continually up into his eyes. He attempted to straighten it, whereupon one of the warders came down and delivered a swinging blow that made him sway.

Soon he must fall. He grew more and more ashen. The ground seemed to rock beneath him. He seemed to be trying to sway with the rhythm. He straightened up--and once more --before falling to the ground.

Tora was allowed to do some darning. She worked eagerly for the first few days, welcoming the change of having some- thing to do; but her enthusiasm for daylong darning was short lived. When Funcke caught her walking round the cell instead of darning, she reprimanded her sharply, accusing her of laziness. Then Tora would think of Solveig and the others who enjoyed the work: she need have no bad conscience for slacking off.

She hid away different colored strands of yarn and, when she was in the mood to work, she filled in the holes with stripes and checks. They brightened up the endless grey--and she was sure that the men would not mind.

The light colored stockings were the best. These she en- joyed, poring over them, matching and rearranging colors and appraising the effect.

One day she discovered that she could work with the different colored threads gathered from the feet of woolen stockings. This proved to be almost as absorbing as painting.

Freyer appeared just as she was putting the finishing touches to her first attempt. She pointed proudly at her work. Freyer peered shortsightedly and nodded approvingly at the purple and grey study of a woman's head. She smiled and continued on her rounds. Tora was delighted with the result of her efforts. She could hardly bear to tear it apart--but this had to be done before she could start on anything new.

She needed more wool, so she asked Funcke if she could be given only colored stockings to repair. "Why?" Tora explained that it was so much more fun to work with color.

After this exchange, she was given only black and grey stockings to repair. What was it that made Funcke so vicious, she wondered. Why deny a prisoner such a trivial pleasure? That she should keep strictly to the rules was understandable-- but to be so mean!

Tora was surprised at what she could accomplish with only black and grey. Working on a man's head one day, she became so absorbed in shaping the ear that she did not hear Black Maria until she was standing in the door. But Black Maria could not see the head of a jaunty man. She saw that the blanket had been removed from the bed and that a heap of dark woolen fluff had been gathered in the middle; she saw that the prisoner was engrossed and happy; she saw the pile of undarned stockings. The warder unleashed a tornado of shouted abuse and banging and flung the wool into a wastebin in the passage. Sadly, Tora resumed her darning. But in the afternoon the ball of fluff was pressed through the spy hole. The prisoner silently blessed the orderly who had thought of her, and set out to create another man's head.

But one day her luck ran out: Funcke entered the cell so unexpectedly that there was no time to conceal the granny face she had been working on. It lay open to view, with innocent grey curls atop a smooth black cape, a bow tied under the chin. The bow fluttered as Funcke's bitter hands wrenched off the head and threw it to the ground. Tora shook; something seemed to shrivel and die within her at that moment. Funcke smiled, a yellow smile of triumph, an evil, yellow smile.

In future Tora was given only underpants to repair. They

were stiff and hard and ugly. Terrible things were happening. A prisoner had hanged himself. Matti's sight had suddenly started to deteriorate. Solveig was in the grip of a deep depression: she was convinced that her mother was dead. Tora felt as though she were being dragged inexorably downwards.

The avalanche was there once more. One day she had seen Larsen among the prisoners on the parade ground. Since this discovery she anticipated more questioning and lived in fearful expectation every day. Just when she had thought that she was free from further interrogation, a key contact had appeared, as large as life!

It was a cruel day. Out of the corner of her eye, Tora looked at a brown jersey lying on the table. There was something about the jersey: she had been ill at ease ever since it had been brought into the cell. It exuded an indefinable something. The male odor and smell of tobacco, that was good; but that other something was strangely evil--it seemed to speak of blood, warm, clotted blood. Freyer had brought it in; Tora had seen it before on one of her friends.

She attempted to repair it, but had to put it aside. Instead, she sat fingering the scissors, testing their sharpness, pressing the points lightly against her wrist. An almost irresistible desire to see blood overcame her. She speculated on how it would feel if she drove the point deep into the artery. She found the spot. She knew that this inexplicable desire sprang from the odor of the jersey. The garment made her uneasy, nervous-- slightly deranged. She could not bear to touch it.

She flung the scissors onto the table and began to pace the floor, praying for delivery from this overpowering sensation of evil. She was not to have peace until Freyer removed it.

Tora spoke to her Lucky Spider. What did she know about the soul? Could it be possible that while we slept, our souls were used elsewhere? She had had the same dream two nights running. The details were identical on both occasions. She dreamt so rarely that when she did, the dream was still clear in her memory when she awoke. She had stood on a vast plain-- in Russia--or China. An old woman was lying in an unpainted wooden crate. Her clothes were in rags and the dry skin on her face was stretched tight over her wide cheekbones. Her eyes were closed. It was evident that she was in pain and about to die.

Tora stood helplessly beside the prostrate figure. She stroked the wrinkled cheeks over and over again. The woman slowly opened her eyes and smiled. The face was serene--the smile marvelously beautiful. Nothing more took place.

She had repaired the stockings; she would not darn the green woolen gloves. She would not--she could not--not after what had happened.

The gloves had been lying on the table for several days. They belonged to one of Freyer's most frequent guests. Funcke pestered her to get finished with them, but she let them lie untouched.

Freyer came to fetch them. She examined them--why were they not finished, had she no wool? Tora showed her the ball of yarn. Why then? The prisoner searched for words. Some days previously she had seen someone with green gloves strike one of the boys. The hand in the green glove had struck with such force that the lad had fallen. There was no hate in her heart for the assailant--but the prisoner was a fellow-countryman, a Norwegian brother--she simply could not. Her eyes brimmed with tears. She looked pleadingly at Freyer

--if she could only understand! The warder took the gloves and left silently.

There was little more lint to be had from stockings: she was given mostly trousers to repair. The small ball she had collected she concealed in her own stockings: Funcke and Black Maria were like hawks.

Now she was making something new. A couple of nails she had found in the compound had given her the idea: she would make a bird--an ostrich. She finished it at dinner time and sat admiring the result. It really wasn't bad--the head was good, the neck long and slender, the body well-proportioned, and no one could see that the fine grey-mottled legs, bound with darning wool, were rusty nails. The cheerful side feathers were her greatest pride, they seemed to literally stand on end.

Surely this could be called art? She smiled and stroked her masterpiece. It was certainly too good for the hard, grasping hands of Funcke and Black Maria. She hid it under her bed until Freyer came, when she explained what it was and asked to be allowed to have it standing on the table. Freyer nodded in assent.

In the evening Funcke appeared and, as she had anticipated, launched into an immediate attack.

"Dolls are not allowed!"

"It's not a doll, it's a bird--an ostrich!"

Tora was confident, waiting to play her trump card. Funcke examined the ostrich.

"What's inside?"

"Bits from my own stockings."

The warder picked at the feathers, recognizing the stocking lint from previous encounters. Her glance fell on the legs. "What's this?"

"Two nails I found in the compound."

"No--the other."

Feigning misunderstanding, Tora willingly showed her the remains of the toothpaste tube she had used to make the bird's feet.

"No, this!"

"Oh that--just ends of darning wool too small to be used for anything else."

Funcke pondered on the useless ends of darning wool; she wasn't quite sure if Tora could have the bird standing there; she would have to ask the head warder.

Tora smiled and gently removed the bird from Funcke's hands. She straightened the feathers, remarking carelessly that in fact she had already asked and been given permission to keep it. It amused her to contemplate the mirror of the warder's face where so much was reflected--not only of Funcke, she felt, but also of what she had grown to perceive as the general Germanic mentality.

Dealing with Black Maria was not so simple: here it was necessary to get in with heavy ammunition at once, before she had a chance to flatten the bird with her clumsy paws. Tora stood protectively in front of the table as she explained. The woman swept her aside, grabbed the precious ostrich by the neck and twisted it around with the motion of wringing a chicken's neck.

Tora was able to salvage the remains and carry out extensive repairs, after which the bird stood unmolested.

A few days later the songbird reappeared. It perched, small and alert, cocking its head and puffing out its breast, ready to begin its song at any moment.

Tora toyed with the notion of converting her cell into a veritable aviary. She imagined the faces of Funcke and Black Maria as they entered and discovered birds everywhere--on the table, the bed, the sink, the window sill, in the cupboard and, beneath the lamp, an effigy of the prisoner herself, swinging from a loop. It was just an idea.

The camp seethed with rumors: they did not merely circulate, but flew like roast chickens into the starving prisoners in their cells: the war was almost at an end; Italy had capitulated; Germany would have to surrender; the final death throes would take at the most a couple of months.

Solveig rejoiced and stitched with renewed vigor at the coat she had taken apart and turned to have something to do. She must have it ready in time for the opening of the gates. The ceiling and walls vibrated with Matti and Kari's peace dance. The prisoners on the parade ground smiled and pointed at their wrists, to the place where they would have worn a watch: soon the hour would come.

The warders continued to beat, castigate, and wreak havoc. Inspections and checks were carried out morning, noon, and night.

Tora took it all calmly, knowing the pattern. The war had been about to end continually during the past six months, always within six months at the most. She had no illusions about the Germans giving up so easily.

She exchanged signals with Solveig, who was totally taken up with the day when they would leave the devils and hell behind them, and with details of their first celebration in freedom, together with Kari and Matti. Tora itched to get back to the latest figure she was working on. For all she cared, the war could go on for five more years now that she was happily engrossed in another creation. The recent harrying of the young men by the Germans had inspired her to make a figure the exact opposite of the Dentzer ideal, a figure which would embody all that the boys were forbidden to be. He would have sloping, drooped shoulders, a curved spine, pot belly, and hands thrust into pockets. She struggled and strove so that a few days later he was sitting, with legs idly crossed, hands in pockets, gazing despondently at the birds. Tora studied him: why she did not know--it had not been her intention--but she saw that he had turned out to be a veritable Italian.

And yet, on second thought, this one--Benito? Of course, he must be called Benito--this one did not resemble any of the Italians she had seen. He had their brown skin and black hair, but his mouth was completely hidden by a drooping black moustache. She suspected that he was toothless--and unusually lazy. Maybe he was one of those who set out, complete with donkey, to cheat the unsuspecting tourist.

She liked Benito. He was not handsome--no--and it was evident that those who saw him, with his lethargic figure, rounded shoulders and soft stomach, felt no immediate attraction; and yet they were compelled to look at him--and finally to like him. Benito was allowed to remain in her cell; the blessing of the head warder had put an effective stop to any spiteful designs on the melancholy, lazy little Italian.

Fourteen

Matti was leaving. Germany, at last! For her, for Solveig, and many others. They had been to a medical examination and knew what this meant. Name lists were hammered from cell to cell, farewell letters circulated.

There was a feverish atmosphere. Most of the single cell inmates were glad of the impending change; anything would be better than the loneliness of isolation. Others were inconsolable one day and signaling optimistically the next, hammering out speculations about internment in large camps for women, camps with wide streets where they would be free to roam.

Tora was paralyzed by the oppressive darkness which always closed in upon her whenever a shipment to Germany was imminent. She had no faith in freedom and wide streets.

One day as she was going about her usual rounds, a vision of Matti suddenly floated before her eyes. She was in the sea and, floating on something, lying with closed eyes, rising and falling in the waves. Tora stood looking at her, awake, and at the same time hearing Matti talking to Kari in the neighboring cell. The spectacle was so vivid that she wanted to stretch out her arms and pull Matti in to land and attempt to revive her. "Matti, Matti! God, think of her mother!"

Night and day Tora prayed--that Matti would not drown,

that Matti would one day return home alive to her mother, or that something would come about to prevent the prisoners from being transported. The vision of Matti in the sea would not go away.

Suddenly, one evening, Tora grew calm; the darkness lifted. It was as though a voice had spoken to her: Trust everything to me. What is best for Matti must happen. Rest assured.

It was a sad morning even so when Solveig and Matti were fetched. In the afternoon Kari was also moved and Tora was alone, with empty cells on either hand. She wanted to cry, but the tears were locked in her breast.

She stood by the window for the remainder of the day, waiting for the trucks to come; but no trucks came.

They would probably come that night. Prisoners were often shipped out at night. She lay awake thinking of Matti's mother, dreading the day when the news reached her.

The night passed; no trucks appeared, nor were the prisoners sent off the following day.

Sunday morning. Tora lay on the floor, her ear to the grating. A greeting from the thirty prisoners who were leaving was read out. They were lined up to march off when the message was suddenly given that departure was postponed.

Tora gave a sigh of relief: now Matti would not drown.

Kari had been placed in a cell at the end of the corridor and shouted a greeting to her. The sound of her voice brought reassurance in the yawning void left by the departure of her neighbors; after they had gone the density of the silence was audible.

She lay on her bed, trying to think of something amusing. It was impossible on that day, when longing for the company of fellow beings racked her entire body. Even the idea of all those prisoners, prostrate on their stomachs, yelling through the gratings, raised no smile; instead, pictures of Solveig and Matti rose up in her mind.

Lord God, why don't we use the time when we have it? Why are we so half-hearted, cold, apathetic? Why don't we love each other?

Why had she not signaled to Solveig, even though her hearing had been poor and she had talked of devils? Why had she not been kinder to Matti?

She lay staring at the ceiling, lines by Øverland reverberating in her brain:

"None can stand by the grave for the rest of a life and mourn.
The day has many hours--the year has many dawns."

The isolation was beginning to affect her nerves. The immeasurable emptiness left by Solveig and Matti.... At last she fully understood the importance of the hammered signals. Even the singing bird had flown away.

The only consolation came from the cell below: the inmates hammered out "good night" through the ceiling every evening. One had a twittering, bird-like voice. Tora often stood at the window listening for that voice. She thought it belonged to a girl called Nancy. A sweet, pure voice--her spirits lifted at the sound.

Something had to be done. She was determined to fight off passivity--as much as was possible. She realized that without her faith, without prayer, she would have lost her reason long since.

She sat lost in thought, toying with a potato, picking idly. It took on the shape of a head and, forgetting the book she was trying to recollect, she began to work--rapidly, nervously. The result was quite different from what she had intended: the head bore more resemblance to the death mask of an old man.

So, it was possible to use potatoes! At last she had discovered a material which they could not take away from her. Tora felt a deep satisfaction, realizing that now she would have something to do, always.

There was nothing in Funcke's list of rules to say that she could forbid a prisoner to pick at a potato. The warder was mildly surprised at the sudden increase in little Halle's appetite: she begged constantly for more potatoes, whereas she had previously pushed them aside. It was a mystery that Funcke never solved.

Tora was enjoying herself: in the cupboard lay four small heads--the heads of her brothers. They shrank daily, the likeness gradually fading, but she hadn't the heart to eat them up.

She would have liked a lump of modeling clay--it would be fun to try. One day, when Tora was out for exercise, Freyer came across the potato heads of a stern grandfather and a cheeky small boy. She lingered, chatting good-naturedly, asking the prisoner if she had done such work outside, if she had been trained. For the rest of the day, Tora felt a happy pride.

The feeling that she must pull herself together, that she could not carry on in the same way, occupied Tora more and more. Her intellect seemed blunted; she had difficulty in concentrating. She was tired and unable to walk as much as before. Her morning prayers took longer and longer. Her thoughts were inclined to slip away towards a vast floating vacuum rather than be put to use; they only wanted peace-- whereas she would have none of that dangerous peace.

What was it that was having the most marked effect? The loneliness or the simple lack of vitamins?

The loneliness was the worst after all. The singing corridor orderly had entered the cell one day and placed her hand on Tora's shoulder. She had stood as though nailed to the floor, quivering, unable to answer the girl's questions--and all because of that hand, even though a faint objectionable smell of the unwashed had hung about the girl.

Tora was shaken to be brought face to face with the physical effect that isolation and bad treatment was having upon her. She had ceased to think about it, so that it was a shock to be confronted by this symptom of reality.

She began to systematically take stock of all she had read; a dismal exercise since she remembered pitifully little--hardly any details but merely the vague impression that each author had given. She allotted one day to each book, only to discover that after about an hour of reflection her thoughts began to wander, straying from one author to another. She let them stray.

Her mind dwelt for the most part on Ibsen. She could still recall the roar of laughter from her classmates when they had once been asked to choose the Ibsen character they would most like to play. "Brand," she had solemnly replied. That roar had made her take a closer look at the Agnes role, and she had come to the conclusion that she could probably play Agnes too --parts of her at least.

She remembered the scene at the vicarage on Christmas Eve and, crossing to the window, began to speak Agnes's lines:

"Shut. Everything is shut.
Even oblivion is shut to me.

I cannot forget, and I am forbidden to weep.
I must go out. I cannot breathe.
In this shuttered room, alone."

She sighed, knowing that she could give a far better performance now than on that earlier occasion, and was lost in thought when the singing orderly suddenly stood in the doorway saying that she was to be moved.

"Moved? Where?"

"Further along the corridor. Kari will be in the next cell," the orderly said, and smiled. Tora was glad to think that Kari would be her neighbor once more. The orderly saw her chance to make a move: the birds--she wanted them--before the others took them. But, hardening her heart, Tora refused; she wanted to give them to Kari.

The consignment for Germany left the same day. It occurred to Tora that Freyer might have moved her on that particular day to spare her from seeing them go. The prisoners always got to know such things in any event, and she was not as distressed as she had been--knowing that Matti would not drown.

The new cell was good enough--a little darker than the previous one but there was a certain intimacy about it: the window sill was covered with signatures--and Kari was nearby. There was more life on every hand. There were three prisoners in each of the adjacent cells and on the other side of the passage seven inmates were in a double cell. Tora felt life pulsing around her and, after the time with no neighbors, the effect was doubly powerful. Her spirits lifted once more.

In the evenings she often lay close to the grating, listening to someone singing in the double cell. The singer had a fine voice, and Tora wished that she would sing every evening in spite of the ache it brought to her heart: she longed for music--and for flowers.

From time to time she smuggled in a flower or a few green leaves from the exercise compound; but they were always detected by Funcke and roughly swept away. She was not even permitted to keep a stray crimson petal in the sink.

It was sometimes difficult to forgive. There was the incident of the paper napkin: the table was so bare and, in an attempt to soften the plain surface, she had torn a scrap of paper from the roll and deftly folded and plaited it into a lacy square. It had taken a lot of work and given a lot of pleasure, and she tried her best to keep it. It was allowed to lie in place until the first outburst was triggered off by something or other--she knew not what. She returned from the exercise compound one day and stood in the doorway, aghast. Black Maria--it could only be she--only she could show such terrifying brutality. The remains of the paper doily lay in a heap in the middle of the table; it had been shredded into minute pieces. The prisoner stood with her coat on, motionless, looking. Funcke would at least have removed the pieces, lessened the pain. Now she felt as though a part of her lay there--destroyed --torn apart by evil hands.

She could not hate. She could not weep. She had been alone for many months, with only God to speak to, to listen to, telling her to love her enemy. At such moments, it was the only thing He had to say.

Tora turned away from the table and swallowed in an attempt to press down the lump in her chest. The cupboard door stood ajar--and she knew before she had looked inside that Benito was gone.

She heard Black Maria in the corridor and pounded on the

door, hammering in a frenzy until the warder appeared. Tora pointed to the heap on the table and softly asked her: "Why had she done it? How could she have done such a thing?" Black Maria laid the blame on Funcke. Her huge hands toyed with her keys, her round childlike eyes avoiding the prisoner's gaze. Later that afternoon, a sizeable parcel was sent to The Fatherland. The day's pillage in the cells had yielded rich booty.

Following this incident Funcke and Black Maria behaved towards Tora with ever increasing spite. She understood. She took up no more petals to her cell. She did not make a new Benito or attempt to fashion more paper lace. The thought of more destruction, theft, slaughter, was more than she could bear.

A new prisoner had come to Kari's cell. Tora was curious, expectant. On Sunday they talked through the gratings and the voice of the new prisoner was so vibrant and clear that the sound all but took her breath away. If the voice was anything to go by, she must be a redhead.

That evening Kari signaled that Inger, the newcomer, had been fetched for questioning at The Terrace. There was no more knocking that night. Tora passed the hours in contemplation and prayer until she heard her being locked into her cell in the morning.

In the afternoon she was fetched once more. From the sound of her footsteps, it seemed that her legs were uninjured. So far. Tora dreaded the coming night. Inger had not slept. "If only they don't beat her, if only they don't put on the screws--spare her from that! Give her the strength to endure, dear God, help her to survive. Give Kari sleep--and help Inger."

The night was long--longer than her own night at The Terrace, which had suddenly come so near. "God in heaven, spare Inger!" She kept up her entreaties as she wandered in her imagination along the dark passages at The Terrace, from cell to cell, trying to find Inger. She was unable to sleep, searching for Inger, whom she had never seen. She would not leave her alone in that cellar, she would share the pain with her. But she could not find Inger.

In the morning she knocked fearfully on the wall: "Has Inger come back?" "No."

The morning passed, but Inger did not return. Where was she? What had they done to her? Maybe she was lying, bruised and bloody, in one of the cold, innermost cells. Maybe at that very moment she was opening her eyes, feeling the cold stone floor and remembering the events of the night. Perhaps they would come to the cell to continue where they had left off. Perhaps she would die--alone and in pain.

Not before the evening did she hear the appointed signal: Inger had returned. She fell asleep, waking some hours later at the sound of keys jangling in the neighboring cell. It was the third night.

Inger was fetched for further questionings, several times over a long period. She was absent for days and nights, occasionally sleeping for an hour or two on rare nights. Tora lived as in a nightmare, praying more intensely than ever before; the unknown Inger dominated her entire world.

Her hair was not red: she was dark and wrote amusing small notes. Tora was now sustained by the letters written by Kari and Inger. The windows had once more been painted over so that there was not even a glimpse of the sky to bring pleasure into their lives.

Instead, she and Kari began to build a cabin in the Vassfaret forest, where the bear roamed silently in the vast wilderness. The evening stillness was deep, awe inspiring, and in the moonlight the shadows of trees took on the shapes of trolls and monsters. Decaying old trunks formed silver-grey bridges over glittering streams. They rambled and strayed, to find their way at last back to the safe warmth of their tent.

Or they would wander along Bygdøy allé on a dark, blustery October evening. The street lamps swung back and forth in the wind as they waded ankle deep in the fallen slippery, shining chestnut leaves. Warm, overripe autumn filled the air.

Sometimes they sailed away to Zanzibar, and there they cultivated cloves and coconut palms. In that rich soil and balmy climate, they gathered in two crops a year. Tora painted or gathered armfuls of sweet smelling blossoms--while Kari struggled with coconuts.

Inger told tales of London--Paris--Vienna. Divine music-- good theater. It was the best time in the cells.

Fifteen

One day she was suddenly told that she was going to be moved. She sent farewell letters to the neighboring cell and folded and refolded her clothes.

The days passed and nothing happened--until one morning Freyer came to tell her to get ready for questioning at The Terrace. For a brief moment the world seemed to stand still.

Tora dressed and lay on her bed, suddenly unable to stand upright. Freyer was not behind her shouting, "Quick, quick!" For this she was thankful, thankful for every minute to prepare herself for the coming ordeal.

She hammered out the word "interrogation" to Kari, needing to be sure that they would be with her in thought when she was at The Terrace. They wanted to know more but she felt incapable of more knocking and lay down again. There was something of greater importance than signaling at this moment: she drew close to her sole support and soon her feeling of helplessness lifted. She felt exhausted yet at the same time completely calm.

The car was full of prisoners. Tora stood for a moment, breathing in the atmosphere around other living beings, the strangeness of being near people once more. There was a deep pleasure in the pressure of the bodies on either hand, warmth and gratification surged through her. She did not experience her companions as men or women, but felt them only as fellow beings, warmblooded, alive. Cautiously she slipped her hands into their hands and felt them enclosed in a gentle clasp. Now, for all she cared, they could drive to the end of the world.

She was astonished to be offered a chair--to sit on! It would have been less surprising if it had been hurled at her head.

"Are you sitting comfortably?"

As she had expected, there was little change.

The grey fellow was morose, palefaced and evidently suffering from early morning doldrums. He hung up his outer garments, transferring a revolver from his topcoat to his trouser pocket as though it were a handkerchief.

He was wearing a different suit, fine material, good cut. The man himself seemed changed too--there was an air of indifference about him.

He read the morning post, glanced at the headlines in a German newspaper, shuffled papers; the prisoner seemed not to exist.

She reflected on how strange it was that one could perspire merely from sitting and waiting.

In a block on the far side of the street, a man stood looking out of a window. She wondered if he knew how fortunate he was.

The telephone rang. "Schubert." The man in grey spoke rapidly for a long time.

Schubert! Sacrilege--he should not have that name! Music welled up inside her, causing her to almost forget where she was. What was it--that music by Schubert? Something to do with death--Death and the Maiden. Death and the Maiden.

A pale, slightly round shouldered man entered. "Heil Hitler!" He approached the desk hesitantly and gave the grey fellow a questioning glance before seating himself.

"Fetch the documents." "Jawohl!" He clicked his heels together lifelessly and sloped off. There was a lifelessness about the whole man. To Tora he appeared to belong to the great Norwegian flock of stray sheep.

The grey one leafed through numerous papers and gave a brief summing up. The case had been cleared up; it was complete; only her confession was lacking and that they were going to get that day, even if it had to be wrung from her. So much wringing had already taken place; how wonderful it would be to confess everything and be finished with it, Tora thought. She braced herself on the chair and sat silently through two hours' interrogation, exhausted, perspiration trickling.

The earlier mood of her interrogator changed to ill-tempered seething. He strode back and forth, finally stopping in front of her and pointing at his watch: she would get fifteen minutes in the basement in which to think the matter over. If she still refused to speak after that time, then he would wash his hands of all responsibility for her future fate. Further torture would be necessary--on order of the highest authority. Was he still not aware of the inhumanity and, in this case, total futility of these methods, she asked. He gave no reply.

The stray sheep nagged at her to get a move on as they descended the stairway. She retorted that after eleven months' incarceration, her knees turned to jelly at the first step; furthermore, she was still paralyzed by the terror of earlier interrogations, even though she had remained untouched throughout this last one, sitting on a chair. She asked if he had ever tried to imagine what it would be like to be confined to a one man cell, alone, with nothing to do, for a year. And how could he, a Norwegian, allow himself to be a part of it all?

To this he had no reply but after her outburst she was now allowed to go at her own pace.

All was quiet in the basement--no sound of screams or swinging whips. But the awareness of what happened and could happen again at any moment hung like an obscure threat in the dank air.

She did not think anything would happen that day. No-- nothing would happen.

And yet why not?

Why should she not trust that voice telling her that nothing would happen on that day?

And in any case, even if something should happen, she would come through. Why should she not manage as well now as she had on the previous occasion? Of course she would --she had some training behind her now. The first time was always the worst. Then the pain had been so intense--it could not possibly be worse. She remembered it all clearly, after all, and she had managed to hold out then.

Yes, but I can't take as much any longer. Nonsense--of course you can!

No--I cannot! Yes, yes--of course.

Harald, if.... Mother--Father--Marit. Marit, take care!

Tora walked back and forth, back and forth.

"Well now, what have you got to say to this?" The man in grey handed her a sheaf of case papers to read, to "help her to get moving," as he put it.

She said nothing. It was as though a part of her had died.

All that the man in brown had said about Leif, it had all been true. She read his entire statement. There was no room for doubt. They would not have fabricated a complete case, filling three large files, for the sole purpose of extracting a confession from her; her evidence was not that important.

She had not been given just one page or any particular pages, but had been allowed to leaf through the entire document and read at will.

Everything was there, totally and painfully accurate. Leif had told them absolutely everything he knew about her.

Why had he told them that she had worked as courier? Surely that at least could have been avoided? He could have just said that she had been an occasional helper.

Uncontrolled rage flared up momentarily within her. It was true what the man in brown had once said to her: "Be sensible--do as Leif Simonsen. He has given a full confession and not a hair on his head has been harmed. He gets his parcels and is allowed to write letters. He is together with several other prisoners, gets dental and medical treatment--and is well treated in every way."

Damn such men--damn them! So much for loyalty! In an all out effort she managed to gain control of her feelings. It was foolish to rail against all men because some gave up.

On the other hand, he need not have surrendered at all: it was impossible to know under what pressure these admissions had been forced. Leif had not known to what extent she had been involved in other directions. He may have imagined her to be only indirectly involved, and given her name to avoid betraying other, more important contacts.

But what about all the others he had named? That doesn't concern you.... She resolved to put him from her mind until that day, sometime in the future, when all would be explained.

Sørholt had managed to hold out.

Larsen's name was not mentioned at all in the papers. They

must have got him in connection with something else. She thought with gratitude of her sister who had managed to get rid of the breadbox and the money. On that account, she was safe--Larsen and Marit too.

Reading through the report had been of no help. She realized that if she let slip one word of the true facts of the case, the entire network would crumble. She ran her eye over Leif's statement once more; she would say that she could take no responsibility for anything he had said, but could only answer for herself.

The grey fellow was patently irritated. The sheep sat looking at him helplessly. "Don't sit there gazing--get on with the statement, for God's sake!" With his round shoulders increasingly bowed, the man made ready. He appeared inexperienced and awkward. Once more she began at the beginning, retelling the tale which by that time must have been all too familiar to the man in grey.

He sat motionless, following closely. The sheep glanced at him nervously from time to time, raising his voice if he seemed irritated, or hitting the table, attempting to emulate his lord and master in every way. He was clearly afraid of him.

Tora was almost enjoying herself--this was nothing compared with the previous interrogations.

The man in grey questioned her about her personal opinion of the National Socialist Party and of the resistance of Norwegians to the occupying power. She replied bluntly that the party was supported by only two percent of the population and that the remainder, regardless of their political views, formed a united block against both the party and the Germans.

The round shouldered fellow squirmed in his chair, evidently not caring to be reminded of the two percent.

"And why is this?" he asked. She saw mounting displeasure

in his face as she attempted to explain.

"Out!" he roared at last, pounding the table with clenched fists. A light cloud of dust rose from the papers.

The round shouldered lackey led her back to the cellars.

Exhausted, she sat in a corner on the stone floor, wondering if she had made a mistake in speaking out. No--it would do them both good to hear it.

It was long past noon and she was beginning to feel hungry; but it was of no importance: the recent experiences were worth more than food. She relived the intense pleasure of the car journey, the good feeling of close, warm bodies, the cautious pressure of hands.

One of the prisoners had had such fine eyes--beautiful, but it was their expression which lingered in her mind: there was no bitterness in their frank gaze.

She recalled his hurried whisper--thirteen months in isolation--was it that which had made him as he was? The puffy skin under his eyes--how many tears had he cried?

Her thoughts were interrupted by a guard unlocking the door and asking if she had been given food. No, she hadn't. He hesitated in the doorway and asked why she had been arrested. She had done no more than her duty to her country. He seemed to turn her reply over in his mind before going on to ask how long she had been interned. She told him how long and about conditions in the prison. She asked him if he were aware of what was going on in that place.

He made no reply; the question seemed of no interest to him. Instead, he drew near to her--nearer. He would fetch food, and a cigarette, he said.

Gently she removed the urgent young hands. He flushed and stammered; was she angry? She looked at him openly, smiled and said no. Relieved, he said that he would come with food as soon as possible, and left.

Maybe her vibrating senses were mirrored too clearly in her appearance on that day. She felt a jubilant happiness because the interrogation had gone so well and because she believed that it was the last she would have to undergo. The guard was so patently young. He had never experienced the isolation of a one man cell. How could he understand her eager hoarding of every impression, every new face, every new voice, that she would live for a long time on every new glance?

She smiled, thinking that he would not understand either that she had not the slightest urge towards the erotic, only an intense longing for tenderness. A wave of warmth and love for Harald suddenly flooded over her. His hands were never greedy; maybe that was why she loved them so. They were alive, warm, their caress filled with goodness and a strange deference. She sat in a corner, closed her eyes to dream of Harald.

"She's asleep. She must be mad!" The voice of the man in grey sounded incredulous. She was not sleeping--she just wanted to escape from prison, back to Harald.

They came over to her and one of them kicked her on the leg. It didn't hurt. She opened her eyes, stretched her limbs, and followed them out.

On the way up from the basement she asked when she would be given food. The grey one replied in a friendly tone: she could have as much food as she liked if she would talk. She told him that conversational skills were lost entirely after six months in isolation; furthermore, she had had nothing to read for eleven months. He told her to shut her damned mouth.

She looked at her other escort, the slow-witted interpreter from Dentzer's office, "the vacuum cleaner," as he was known to the boys. A descriptive epithet: as he sloped around with dangling arms, his head jutting out half a yard before his body, his appearance did recall to mind some half forgotten advertisement for a vacuum cleaner.

She shivered as she climbed the steps, feeling a clamminess about her body. The vacuum cleaner made an attempt at questioning her. She asked him, did he not remember her story from their previous encounter, in Dentzer's office? She was tired and hungry; there was no point in talking any more.

"D'you think that the NS and the Germans are going to be duped by a slip of a girl like you? D'you think I'm stupid?" He struck the table--rubbing his knuckles afterwards.

The urge to answer in the affirmative was tempting, but she behaved as though he did not exist; this irritated him.

He worked his way through various degrees of anger, finally leaping to his feet and shaking her by the shoulders, screaming, "Answer, for God's sake!"

On that day, although she did not understand why, Tora felt herself to be in possession of extraordinary strange strength and composure. She brushed her shoulder lightly where he had grasped her and asked, what was it he had said?

The interrogation was at an end. The vacuum cleaner said that he had to go to a meeting but was told to note down the prisoner's personal details first. This done, she was led down to the cellar for the third time.

The guard did not bring food as he had promised. Tora paced back and forth to keep warm, her hands blue-mottled with cold. Were they going to keep her there all night? This she dreaded and wished she were back in her solitary cell. She heard the door being unlocked.

"So you're still alive, then?" The pale youth who had been present as a handwriting expert at her first interrogation was sneering at her.

"You too?" She could not forget his laughter when she had prayed that night.

Halfway up the stairs she had to rest. He told her to be sensible and confess that night.

Her heart stopped: "Tonight," he had said.

She suggested that they speak of something else--how were things going on the Eastern Front, for example? He made no further attempt at conversation as they resumed their climb.

The grey fellow was in an almost human mood. After an hour's fruitless attempt to get something out of her he took out her first and only statement; it covered half a side of a sheet of paper. She fixed her eyes on the bottom line where he had added: "Working against the German defense force and the National Assembly on patriotic grounds." That at least was true.

She signed. The man in grey read it through, shaking his head: he would be a laughing stock for sending in a document like this. What about all those names they should have had!

She did not respond. She had a feeling that at last it was all over, a feeling of happiness and of peace. The nightmare was over! She had managed it and could have wept with thankfulness.

The man in grey read her statement through once again, still shaking his head. Finally, he looked at her questioningly and in broken Norwegian said, "Tora, Tora, why won't you talk?" Once more this question was met with silence.

"Herr Schubert." He looked up quickly from the papers he was arranging. "Do you remember the two nights when I was here last?" His features took on the hard Gestapo manner, his voice was cold. "Yes."

"Since this is probably the last time I shall see you, I just want to say that if at any time in the future you should feel a need for forgiveness, you have mine."

His mouth opened and he remained sitting, with a foolish expression on his face. He closed his mouth, drew his chair closer to the table at which she was sitting, and asked her to repeat slowly what she had said. She did so, as distinctly as possible. He stared at her without uttering a word.

As the group of prisoners stood lined up at the exit, the young guard approached and whispered in a woebegone voice, "I didn't forget the food--I wasn't allowed to bring it!"

There were five more prisoners in the group so that there was no room for a guard in the back of the van. Tora quickly found a place on the lap of the boy who had been inside for thirteen months. One of the new prisoners attempted a snide joke. This Tora ignored; nothing should spoil the day for her; and yet it stung for she had completely forgotten the ways of the world.

She made allowances for the new prisoner--he could have no idea of the effects on the mind of confinement in a solitary cell--and crept closer into the arms surrounding her. There she was safe: the unknown prisoner had a deeper understanding of humanity than the jokester so recently removed from freedom.

They spoke in low voices of their experiences, of how the day had been for them--and were agreed that the war would soon be over.

He pushed something into her pocket. Two cigarettes! She checked a sudden impulse to kiss him; the others would think she had gone mad.

An old man offered her a slice of bread. She gave him a wide smile and began to chew energetically to please him; she was no longer in the least hungry and the slice was unappetizingly thick--but the old man was kind and touchingly eager to share what he had.

They were all kind. Her eyes filled with tears as she chewed at the hard, dry stump.

They had arrived. She did not want to let go of his hand and to be alone once more.

They stood waiting beside the van. Soon they must drop hands. She felt an urge to hide in his arms, let all the loneliness be washed away in tears, close in those arms. She was not conscious of him as a man but solely as a human being who had shared her experiences--a fellow creature who knew and understood.

Tora whistled softly as she hung up her clothes and washed. She was touched that the girl on the corridor should have remembered her food: three large potatoes and a tin can of fish had been placed on the radiator. Apparently they thought she needed extra food after her ordeal.

It was silent in the corridor. The prisoners had gone to bed long since. Suddenly Kari hammered out a signal: they wanted to use the sling. She hastily scribbled down an account of the day's events, wound it around one of the cigarettes, and gave the three-knock signal, hoping that the guard would wait a little before coming to check.

All went well on this occasion. When Funcke came on her

inspection round, Tora sat innocently eating fish and was allowed to keep the light burning for an extra fifteen minutes.

The stocking was a veritable cornucopia that evening. A fine red apple--wherever they had managed to get hold of such a thing --lay carefully hidden under her pillow. She tried to eat the fish with her nose turned towards the tempting, fresh smell from the bed. An apple--an apple!

The meager contents of the cupboard had been supplemented by a jar of face cream and a welcome letter, written on pink paper handkerchiefs.

After a time, reaction began to set in. She pushed the fish away, nauseous from the smell; her hands trembled and perspiration broke out over her body as she spelled her way laboriously through the letter, listening for Funcke's footfall.

Something bad had happened on her corridor while she had been away: seven prisoners had been moved. The others assumed that they had been sent to Germany and Kari had ended her letter with "Your name was called too, Tora. Aren't you glad you were at The Terrace and escaped being sent?"

Tora hummed softly as she undressed. She was happy, happier than she had ever been since her imprisonment. But not because she thought she had escaped being sent to Germany; a triumphant happiness surged through her because now she knew that she had stood the test; what happened to her hereafter was of less importance.

She smiled as she lay in the dark. What fear should she have for the future when the good Lord had been with her all through this harrowing time? She thought of the cold cell at The Terrace and crept further down into the warmth of the bed. She thought of how the day could have ended, in suffering and torture, and fell into a deep sleep in silent thanks for the close of the day.

Some days later Funcke appeared in the morning and said that she should pack her things.

"Does this mean that I'm going to be set free?" She had difficulty in making progress with her packing, a dull numbness seemed to pervade her body.

Funcke's manner was formal, strange, and Tora understood it was not freedom that lay ahead. "I know nothing, only that you are leaving. Freyer will be here later--ask her," she said.

Tora made an effort to carry on with her packing. How would she manage to say goodbye to Kari and Inger?

Funcke took over the packing. The prisoner fumbled, hands trembling. She took out the warmest garments and told the prisoner to dress well, saying that it was cold outside.

Tora ceased to speculate but finished dressing and seated herself on the edge of the bed.

Freyer appeared. "What does this mean? Where am I going? Am I going to be set free?" "It's possible. I only know that you have to call in at The Terrace. Prisoners who are going to be let out often have to call in there to collect their papers." Freyer's smile was strange, in a way sad and reflective.

Tora looked at her, trying to penetrate far behind the spectacle lenses to the truth.

No, it was not freedom that awaited her. Neither Funcke nor Freyer would have behaved as they did. The faint glimmer of hope died.

"To Germany?" As far as she knew no woman had been sent down there alone--at least not from Grini.

Kari--Inger! Tora coughed loudly as she passed their door on her way down.

She stood in an office for a long time, waiting for what was alleged to be the contents of her handbag. She enquired about the money, her pen, a gold bangle, gloves, the handbag itself and a briefcase which had also not been returned. A red-headed fellow in German uniform came to fetch her. She asked him if he would tolerate being robbed in such a manner, to which he replied in a faultless rural dialect that she should stop thinking about things and be glad to get out of the place.

An old German spoke up, took a note of the missing articles and sent a messenger with it to the women's section.

The redhead placed a paper before her to be signed. She read with astonishment that on release the prisoner was bound by law to maintain complete secrecy on all events that had taken place during internment. She flung the paper away, refusing to sign. "A promise like this could never be kept!"

"In which case you'll have to remain sitting here." "That won't bother me in the least--I've already been sitting for so long that a few hours more or less won't make the slightest difference."

"Damn you, woman, don't you understand that I'm busy!" He stormed out, slamming the door so that the walls shook.

The old German disappeared into an adjoining room. A prisoner's head suddenly appeared in an opening to the records room. He whispered rapidly, "Sign it! It's just a formality. Even if you don't get out, you're bound to be better off than here, wherever you end up."

The German returned and after a while Funcke appeared with her gloves and briefcase.

Tora asked where the watch and her handbag were--and the money, all the money she had in the world. "Can you imagine anything so low, Frøken Funcke, imagine--stealing--

over a hundred kroner!" She smiled inwardly, thinking of all the millions being stolen by the Germans daily. The warder turned and said that she would look for the watch and handbag once more.

The redhead came back, glanced at the paper and pushed a pencil into her hand.

She hesitated. It was not right, even if they had described it as no more than a formality. She placed the pencil on the table. The prisoner peering through the opening in the wall motioned to her to sign. The redhead yelled in exasperation, "Sign it for God's sake! All it means is that you don't have to tell that this one's in that cell or that that one's in another cell!" Reluctantly, she signed. He breathed a sigh of relief.

Funcke appeared with the watch and the bag. As she was about to leave, Dentzer entered the room.

"So, still not talking?" She made a remark to the effect that a life spent in isolation did little to develop the ability to talk.

"Well, here at least you have the chance to confide in someone in your own language. He's Norwegian." He indicated the redhead.

"He? Norwegian? In that uniform?" She gazed from one to the other.

The redhead shifted uncomfortably and mumbled that they must be off, his time was running short. Overhearing this, she told Dentzer about the stolen money. She would never get it back--she knew that--but she was determined that he too should know about the theft.

He looked at her with an ironical, appraising gaze; he was sure that she would get it back when she got to The Terrace.

The prisoner in the wall opening raised his left eyebrow briefly. She smiled at him before leaving.

A green police car was drawn up outside. It was evident that the redhead did not like her. He slammed the car's back door firmly after her, preferring to sit beside the driver. Slowly the car rolled out through the gateway.

Epilogue

Sigrid Heide wrote a second part to her story of the war years. It documents her imprisonment in Germany, the degradation, and the mistreatment she suffered and witnessed Allied civilian prisoners suffer in Germany's concentration camps.

As the Allies landed in France and as the Russians advanced from the east, Sigrid Heide (Tora) and all the prisoners heard the air attacks on Berlin in the distance. But the chaos increased, and the death rate continued to rise, right up to the end.

Transported to Akershus Fortress, Tora became part of a group of five Norwegian women who would be shipped to Germany together. They were gathered for the trip late at night. The fortress was bathed in moonlight.

As the women were counted for the last time and moved off, they caught a final glimpse of Oslo, spread out like a ghost town, silent in the moonlight. The only sound they heard was the tramping of their own feet.

The ship loomed like a huge grey wall alongside the dock.

The five women were locked far forward in the bow of the ship, in a room hardly bigger than a closet. Tora protested that

183

it wasn't legal to hold prisoners in such a way, especially since the Germans knew the ship could be the victim of a mine at any time. Trapped below, behind locked doors, the prisoners' life belts were useless.

Tora's fears were realized when the ship ran into an Allied minefield. The ship stopped, surrounded by explosions, while the Germans cleared the water of mines. The women sat quietly as the floors and walls of their floating cell shook.

Allowed on deck once for air, a guard pointed out to Tora something that resembled a narrow strip of a dark cloud. It was her last glimpse of Norway, perhaps forever.

The ship she and her companions were on was part of a convoy of seven troopships on its way to occupied Denmark.

Tora and the other prisoners were unloaded at Aarhus, a town on the east coast of Denmark's Jutland peninsula. They went by rail from Aarhus to Kiel, their first stop in Germany.

Compared to the neat Danish town, Kiel was dirty and lifeless. The railroad station had been bombed, and other traces of war were apparent to the prisoners. Individual houses were in ruins; elsewhere whole blocks had been destroyed.

For the five Norwegian women, entering their first German prison was like entering a cackling farmyard. The prison was filled with babbling, screaming, laughing cursing women. A loathsome stench met them at the open door to the prison courtyard.

To Tora, the deepest shock of all was the sight of the sores--putrid, running, encrusted sores on everyone--and the filth that contributed to them.

Tora and the other Norwegian women experienced their

first air raids at that prison. Bombs hit the ground with dull thuds. Hysterical screams from neighboring cells accompanied each explosion. Though they suffered seven air raids in three days, no bombs actually fell on the camp.

After a medical examination, where many younger women were fondled by the doctor, Tora was transferred to a prison in Neumunster, just south of Kiel.

Compared to the camp at Kiel, conditions at Neumunster were cleaner, more comfortable. But forty prisoners were herded into each room.

From there, the Norwegian women were sent on the next stage of their journey by train. On their arrival, they were herded like cattle to the open German countryside, near Neubrandenburg.

About seventy-five miles north of Berlin, Neubrandenburg was an attractive little town, clean and unscarred by bomb craters. Here, as in other towns, the population was mostly women.

Besides digging an air raid shelter for the town, the Norwegian women spaded the mayor's garden. They often received sympathy from the townspeople because King Haakon VII had fled Norway with the Norwegian gold reserves, avoiding being captured by the Germans in 1940. His escape left Norway without a leader, according to the German point of view.

The mayor thought the king should have at least left the gold. The townspeople didn't understand that the king was Norway's symbol of resistance to German aggression.

While digging in the mayor's garden, Tora enjoyed seeing chickens again. In lighter moments, she wondered if German hens stood in orderly rows on their perches, cackling in unison.

In April 1944, Tora was pushed through the gate to the concentration camp of Ravensbrück, northeast of Berlin. More than one hundred Norwegian women ended up there. They were among 120,000 prisoners from all of Europe who were transported there during the war.

Tora was one of six hundred so-called N.N. political prisoners. This group was to receive especially rough treatment as slave workers until they collapsed in "Nacht und Nebel" (night and fog).

The beatings, the kicks, the overcrowded blocks of green cement houses, the hunger, and the terrible smells in Ravensbrück soon made Tora look back with longing on the time she was a prisoner in Norway.

After eating nondescript breakfasts of thin soup, Tora and the other prisoners followed the same daily routine. They were marched to a factory where they cut used fur coats into pieces, laced the pieces of fur into bundles, and piled them up at a fast and furious pace late into the evening.

Other women prisoners were used by the Germans as draft animals, pulling heavy wagons with bowed backs.

At Nazi inspections of the women prisoners, the German inmates' names were always called first, the Norwegians second, and the Russians last. The Russians were called last and treated the worst because they weren't considered to be Aryan.

Prisoners were stripped of almost all their possessions, permitted to keep only a toothbrush, a comb, and soap. Tora pleaded with two uniformed guards to allow her to keep a small photograph of Harald, but the picture was snatched away.

There were endless lines to be deloused.

Polish, French, German, Russian, Dutch, and Norwegian languages were heard throughout the camp.

The prisoners were very parochial. French prisoners didn't want Norwegians sharing their water; Polish prisoners threatened Russians who attempted to use their possessions. In general though, the Norwegians were admired throughout the camp for their cleanliness and for their honesty.

Tora was called a "Schmuckstück" by a guard. Later she learned the term was used to describe the worst looking individuals in the camp.

In turn, the prisoners dubbed the camp superintendent "Greymouse."

The days passed. Prisoners learned to stand in line for everything and to accept that their bunks were narrow, uncomfortable, and crawling with fleas and lice. They learned how to dress and undress lying in those bunks, out of the way of the traffic in the aisles. They learned the wisdom of keeping their soap in their hands and their garments around their necks when washing. They learned to stow boots, clothes, soap, and food under their pillows.

Tora had been in the hospital block with diarrhea and influenza for eight days. The first three days, she was fed a diet of evil-tasting barley soup until, mercifully, it ran out.

Tora's fever continued, but she chose to return to work. It was better to be at work. The hospital was full of lice, and the stench of living skeletons was disgusting.

She sweated through the nights, shivered through the morning roll calls, and stood through the torture of the eleven-hour work days. Tora was unable to keep down the lumps of gritty cabbage the prisoners were fed for dinner. She consoled herself with the realization that she didn't have typhoid or tuberculosis, like many of the prisoners did. It didn't seem to matter that she was too exhausted to speak.

Even in the brightest sunshine, the days were grey, the camp was grey, the prisoners were grey. Tora seemed to drift in an endless sea of grey.

She saw the block commandant rip shawls and belts from prisoners' bodies. She saw Greymouse gloat as she lashed out, and she saw skeletons collapse into pools of brown filth. The bodies stayed there until roll call ended.

Tora saw more clearly than ever before the prisoners' desperate eyes crying out for affection or mercy. She, herself, had lost the spark of life with which to respond. The spark had been clubbed to death.

Both the Danish Red Cross and Swedish Red Cross sent food parcels to the Norwegian women, but the recipients had to guard them with their lives.

One evening, three bread rations had been stolen. Fifty enraged prisoners ransacked bundles and boxes, straw bedding and pillows, their own and others'. Voices drowned one another in screams and accusations in at least five different languages. They grabbed each other by the hair. Bodies crept, crawled and hurled themselves over kicking legs and gasping skeletons. Suddenly, there was a shout. The thief had been found.

As a prisoner, Tora never met a German woman who could not be bribed, whether guard or prisoner. The German prisoners were either criminals or prostitutes and had no scruples about informing against both foreigners and their own countrymen. The Germans seemed to fear one another more than the prisoners of other nationalities.

The prisoners' sweated profusely.

Tora dragged and heaved the bale. A pain stabbed at her heart and the bale fell to the ground. A guard shouted at her, but she was not able to hoist it to her shoulder again and was forced to carry it in her arms.

It was impossible to throw it high enough. She tried once, twice, over and over again before straightening up, wiping the sweat from her eyes.

The guard laughed. "Once more," he shouted, watching her with his hands behind his back, rocking back and forth with legs apart. Tora tried once more, to no avail.

"Stick at it!" he roared. She grasped the bundle and flung it to the floor with such violence that a cloud of dust arose. She quivered with rage and longed to hurl herself onto the towering, scrawny, laughing guard.

She shouted that it was barbaric to force starving women to do heavy men's work while healthy, grown men stood with their hands behind their backs, looking and laughing. Past all caring, she waited for him to strike.

Nothing happened. He did not hit her. He laughed, and laughed, and tossed the bale lightly into place.

He grinned whenever he saw her for the rest of the day.

Numbers and names were being called out. The prisoners went to Greymouse's table and came back with green paper slips. When it was Tora's turn, Greymouse explained that, though Tora was lazy, she would be given some slips because she was Norwegian. Tora could exchange the slips for food in the canteen.

Tora refused them. Her refusal was regarded as sabotage. Greymouse was astonished that Tora would not accept payment for slavery. Other Norwegian prisoners thought she was being foolish and putting them all at risk.

Good God, are they still standing there? Tora's weary steps flagged as they passed two thousand new prisoners who had been standing outside for three days. SS men saw to it that the new arrivals weren't approached or helped by any of the camp's inmates.

The new prisoners stood or sat all day long, crying out for water. At night, they huddled together on the dew-soaked ground, attempting to keep the night chill at bay by warming each other.

Many were clad in rags. All were unbelievably filthy.

Tora was shaken by the laughter and chatter of the inmates as they passed this mass of exhausted, starving, thirsting, wailing creatures. They had lost all sympathy, all human emotional response.

Silenka, the SS man who was in charge of the women, went beserk almost every day. He was quite young, with a slim, well-trained body. His face would have been handsome had it not been for the fanatical, slightly mad light in his eyes and his hard, cruel mouth.

He loved to strike women to the ground and enjoyed punching a young girl's face with his clenched fist and seeing the blood spurt from her nose. His most recent victim had been an eighteen-year-old, well-built Russian girl. She had fallen to the ground without a sound.

Tora had been appointed louse-exterminator in the N.N. block. For four days a week, Tora stood in the washing room, crushing lice. The crackling sound and sight of the blood collecting under her thumbnails were just as repulsive on the fourth day as they had been on the first.

Many of the Poles in the block were so-called guinea pigs because of the experiments carried out on them by a German doctor. Over one hundred prisoners, for the most part young and in good health, were selected.

In spite of their protests, they were subjected to a series of experiments at the hospital. The chief physician carried out numerous operations on legs and thighs, taking bone samples, removing muscles and sinews, and studying the effects of untried ointments.

Those who refused to get on the operating table were removed by force to an underground cell. The operations would be carried out there, without any form of anesthetic.

The weeks passed and Christmas 1944 approached. Each day brought penetrating wind, rain, or sleet. The prisoners were half soaked and continually cold. The number of prisoners in the N.N. block increased to a thousand. Night air raids became more and more frequent. Two air raid shelters were dug in the loose sand, but they caved in constantly. The prisoners never set foot inside them.

Finally, two thousand prisoners, including Tora and sixteen or seventeen other Norwegian women, were to be transported out of Ravensbrück. They were crowded into shabby railroad cars, seventy women in each one. For five days they were locked in, standing.

The prisoners were pulled out of the cattle cars at Linz, Austria, and driven on foot through the winter slush to the concentration camp at Mauthausen.

It was purely accidental that Sigrid Heide (Tora) and the other Norwegian women escaped from Mauthausen in spring, 1945. Two of them learned that the few Norwegian men in the camp were to be released to the Swedish Red Cross. Sigrid Heide made up a list of the Norwegian women, and the list was smuggled by the men to the doctor on one of the Swedish Red Cross white buses. He didn't have space for the women at that time, but he returned later to Mauthausen and the women were released to him.

They passed through occupied Denmark on their way to neutral Sweden, where Sigrid Heide received a sample of what lay ahead in Norway. She overheard the comments of Swedish moviegoers who had seen a documentary film shot at Bergen-Belsen, an infamous Nazi concentration camp. The Swedes had laughed out loudly, saying that there had to be a limit to such "devilish Allied propaganda." She experienced similar disbelief upon her return to Norway.

Sigrid Heide remembered the mounds of lifeless corpses and the millions of living skeletons released from prison camps throughout Germany. For that holocaust, for that great destruction of life, there was no possible atonement. Not by one generation. Not even by ten generations.

It was only possible to forgive.
But it must never be forgotten because the holocaust has surfaced again.